LEADING
With
Teacher Emotions
IN MIND

To my inspiring mother, Eva Ruth Beatty, née Sawyer

—Brenda Beatty

LEADING
With
Teacher Emotions
IN MIND

KENNETH LEITHWOOD • BRENDA BEATTY

CORWIN PRESS
A SAGE Company
Thousand Oaks, CA 91320

For information:

Corwin Press
A SAGE Company
2455 Teller Road
Thousand Oaks, California 91320
www.corwinpress.com

SAGE Ltd.
1 Oliver's Yard
55 City Road
London EC1Y 1SP
United Kingdom

SAGE India Pvt. Ltd.
B 1/I 1 Mohan Cooperative
   Industrial Area
Mathura Road, New Delhi 110 044
India

SAGE Asia-Pacific Pte. Ltd.
33 Pekin Street #02-01
Far East Square
Singapore 048763

Printed in the United States of America.

Library of Congress Cataloging-in-Publication Data

Leithwood, Kenneth A.
Leading with teacher emotions in mind/Kenneth Leithwood, Brenda Beatty.
    p. cm.
Includes bibliographical references and index.
ISBN 978-1-4129-4144-0 (cloth)
ISBN 978-1-4129-4145-7 (pbk.)
    1. Educational leadership. 2. Teacher-administrator relationships. 3. Teachers—Job stress. 4. Motivation in education. I. Beatty, Brenda (Brenda R.) II. Title.

LB2805.L363 2008
371.2'02—dc22   2007026275

This book is printed on acid-free paper.

        08   09   10   11   10   9   8   7   6   5   4   3   2

Acquisitions Editor:	Elizabeth Brenkus
Managing Editor:	Arnis Burvikovs
Editorial Assistants:	Ena Rosen, Desirée Enayati
Production Editor:	Eric Garner
Copy Editor:	Paula L. Fleming
Typesetter:	C&M Digitals (P) Ltd.
Proofreader:	Carole Quandt
Indexer:	Molly Hall
Cover Designer:	Tracy Miller
Graphic Designer:	Scott Van Atta

Contents

Acknowledgments

We are indebted to several organizations for their support of our work and in particular, collection of the evidence that was used as the foundation for this book. The Elementary Teachers' Federation of Ontario sponsored the initial review of literature on which much of Chapters 2 through 5 are based. The Wallace Foundation funded the large five year study of leadership and learning which was the source of many of the examples and illustrative quotes which appear throughout the book. And Canada's federal Social Sciences and Humanities Research Council funded much of the research underlying the transformational orientation to leadership and the teacher–recalled experiences with their leaders in Chapters 7 and 8 and 9. The international principal online discussion forum was sponsored by the University of Waikato in New Zealand. The contributions of all of the participants in these studies, is much appreciated.

Corwin Press gratefully acknowledges the contributions of the following reviewers:

Mary Alice Barksdale, Associate Professor
Virginia Polytechnic Institute and State University
Blacksburg, VA

Chuck Bonner, Assistant Principal
Great Valley High School
Malvern, PA

Kate A. Foley, Director of Student Services
Lakewood City Schools
Lakewood, OH

Ruth Harper, Professor
Counseling and Human Resource Development
South Dakota State University
Brookings, SD

Lila Jacobs, Professor and Coordinator
Urban Leadership Program
California State University–Sacramento
Sacramento, CA

Kenneth Killian, Assistant Professor
School of Education
Vanguard University of Southern California
Costa Mesa, CA

Lawrence Kohn, Principal
Atascocita High School
Humble, TX

Jerry Vaughn, Principal
Central Elementary School
Cabot Public Schools
Cabot, AR

About the Authors

 **Kenneth Leithwood** is professor of educational leadership and policy at the Ontario Institute for Studies in Education of the University of Toronto, Canada. His research and writing concerns school leadership, educational policy, and organizational change. Dr. Leithwood has published more than 70 referred journal articles and authored or edited more than 30 books. For example, he is the senior editor of both the first and second *International Handbook on Educational Leadership and Administration* (Kluwer Publishers, 1996, 2003). His most recent books (all with Corwin Press) include *Making Schools Smarter* (3rd edition, 2006) and *Teaching for Deep Understanding* (2006). Among his current research projects is a large, five-year Wallace Foundation study, with colleagues, aimed at determining how state, district, and school-level leadership influences student learning. Dr. Leithwood is the recent recipient of the University of Toronto's Impact on Public Policy award and a Fellow of the Royal Society of Canada.

 **Brenda Beatty** is designer and director of the highly regarded Monash Master in School Leadership and the Mentoring for First-Time Principals and Human Leadership: Developing People programs, delivered on behalf of the Victoria State School (Australia) Department of Education. Dr. Beatty is a senior lecturer for the faculty of education at Monash University–Clayton in Victoria, Australia. She lectures and conducts research on the emotions of leadership, leadership development, school improvement, creating collaborative cultures, organizational change, student sense of connectedness and well-being at

school, and the use of face-to-face and interactive Web-based technologies to support the development of professional learning communities. As an international scholar, guest lecturer, and keynote speaker, she has presented her work in China, Ireland, England, New Zealand, the United States, Canada, Australia, and Italy and—via the net-based meeting system WebEx—at various other national and international conferences. Born in Canada and a doctoral graduate of the Ontario Institute for Studies in Education of the University of Toronto, Canada, where she worked with Professor Andy Hargreaves, her research is published in various refereed journals, and her chapter in *The Essentials of School Leadership* is entitled "Emotional Leadership." Various forthcoming publications will consider theories of learning for leadership development, emotional epistemologies, the development of leaders for the future, and the role of emotion in sustaining leader well-being. Dr. Beatty's doctoral dissertation, *Emotion Matters in Educational Leadership: Examining the Unexamined,* won the Thomas B. Greenfield award for best Canadian doctoral dissertation of the year in educational administration. Dr. Beatty is currently working to develop national and international knowledge exchange and support systems to assist local communities anywhere in the world to increase social capital and social cohesion through the development of dynamic, functional, mutually beneficial learning communities.

CHAPTER ONE

Teacher Emotions, School Reform, and Student Learning

A Leadership Perspective

THE PROBLEM

You know, I really love being a teacher . . . wouldn't want to do anything else. Nothing beats the feeling you get when one of your kids finally "gets" something, or you meet a kid years later and she tells you what an influence you had on her life. But . . . like . . . does it have to be such a struggle to actually teach? I mean, really, take this week—I had to collect money being raised by the school for a local charity, fill in a bunch of forms about an immigrant student who had just arrived (that makes 32 in my class, by the way). I was on bus duty morning and afternoon every day. And the principal told us we had to spend at least three hours prepping kids for the state exams next week. They have basically nada—zilch—to do with the curriculum we are teaching this term. Which seems a bit ironic because it is the new curriculum the superintendent has been beating the drums about for the past year (which, by the way, I don't think is as good as the old one). We had parent interviews two nights, which kind of did away with time for marking kids' assignments, so I guess this weekend is shot. Tell you

> *the truth, I'm a bit stressed out. Being a teacher is supposed to be about the kids, but sometimes it just feels that no one is willing to help you do that the best way you know how. It could depress you if you let it—which I try not to.*

The negative emotions expressed by this otherwise optimistic teacher—let's call him Patrick—are hardly atypical or difficult to appreciate. Yet critics routinely dismiss teacher complaints about their working conditions and the emotions associated with them as "just excuses" for not getting on with the task of shaping up our public schools. Reformers typically look past these "distractions," alleging that teachers really need to focus on hard capacities (skills) to deliver the reformers' latest amazing new classroom innovation. (Data walls today—tomorrow, who knows?) And many school administrators have been interpreting teachers' cries for attention to their working conditions as simply irrational "resistance to change" for as long as we (the authors) have been listening—which is a pretty long time.

We beg to differ. We argue that teacher emotions, rather than being excuses, distractions, and knee-jerk resistance, are a potent and largely untapped resource, which educational leaders need to understand better if they are to be directly and intentionally helpful to their teaching colleagues in the shared task of improving student learning.

Let's speculate a bit further about those sources of Patrick's sentiments that could not be fully captured in the short quotation. If he is our "everyteacher," the following picture of his working conditions would not be at all far-fetched:

- Thirty or more students, including a large handful struggling to learn the language of instruction and a similar number with some form of physical or mental disability
- Very limited access to instructional technology and almost no IT support for the technology that is available
- Expectations of some parents to have a very strong influence on his work—and other parents with no expectations of any sort about the school or their children
- A sharp new principal (the third in the last six years) with a strong need to put her own imprint on the school and very little inclination to listen to individual staff members' concerns

- District staff who make frequent demands upon the principal and her staff through memos and e-mails but who have not actually been seen in the school in living memory
- An education bureaucracy and its political masters with a desperate need to be seen in the media to have done something noteworthy within a four-year electoral cycle, resulting in a lot of policy churn, at least "out there," with almost no protection for the teacher from that churn by district or school leaders
- A set of externally set standards that all students are expected to achieve, no matter their starting points, financial resources, parental expectations, or personal motivation
- An external testing system whose results are interpreted as if the only people responsible for students' achieving those standards are teachers and school administrators
- An expectation that this can all be done with no increase in resources, in most cases, and even fewer resources, in some cases

In the United States, much of this picture has been painted by the architects of the No Child Left Behind legislation. Might a teacher feel just a teensy bit out of sorts under these conditions? Do you think?

The conditions under which teachers are being expected to work (the "problem") too often seem akin to a doctor's being asked to do triple-bypass heart surgery with a dull kitchen knife and no anesthetic. And we believe the root cause of these circumstances is a massive failure of leadership—widespread leadership breakdown at many different levels over a very long period of time. Certainly the circumstances we describe as hardly uncommon are almost completely beyond the control of teachers. Some teacher circumstances arise from leadership neglect, mismanagement, and even mistreatment at the school level, while others are the responsibility of those occupying leadership roles in district or state offices; elected officials at the district, state, and federal levels also have to bear a large proportion of responsibility for teacher circumstances.

Toward a Solution

So it is well overdue that we stopped explaining ineffective school reform as a "teacher problem," or only a teacher "ability" problem, and squarely faced the neglected responsibilities of leadership writ large. Of course, teachers often aren't as effective as we might like them to be. But why? Our answer (or "solution") involves the conditions of their work and the responsibility leaders have for deliberately making a difference in those conditions. More specifically, with a focus on school-level leadership, here is the argument we develop in this book:

- Teachers' practices and the learning of their students are significantly influenced by their professionally relevant internal states (thoughts and feelings).
- Because teaching is such an emotionally intense form of work—it is often referred to as "emotional labor"—emotions have a huge influence on what teachers do, even though school reform efforts and many leaders mainly perseverate on teachers' narrowly defined "knowledge" and "skill."
- There is a well-known set of emotions (e.g., morale, stress, commitment) that are elicited by teachers' work, and those emotions are significantly influenced by the conditions of that work, conditions highly influenced by leadership.
- Leaders have been slow to appreciate how powerful a force emotions are in determining what teachers do, and they have exercised their leadership in ways that often provoke negative, rather than nourish positive, emotions.
- However, practices associated with transformational approaches to leadership typically elicit positive emotions on the part of teachers.

Our book, in sum, addresses a longstanding neglect[1] on the part of school leaders regarding the emotions of teachers. It offers guidance to school leaders about how they can become much more effective by paying attention to teacher emotions. It provides recommendations about the exercise of practices associated with transformational approaches to leadership. Attention to emotions (and values) makes this orientation to leadership distinctive from many competing models (Yukl, 1994), especially those concerned primarily with "rational" processes.

---

1. We have enormous sympathy for most school leaders who struggle mightily on behalf of their students and staff. We may sometimes seem critical of their work, and we are certainly asking them to think about it in a more complex way. But our criticism is meant to be helpful and begins from a foundation of great respect.

Emotionally Responsible Leadership

Transformational leadership shines a spotlight on the affective world of organizational members—teacher emotions, in the case of this book—on the basis that this inner world plays a critical role in making teachers' work meaningful. In his foundational work, Burns (1978) argued that transforming leadership "occurs when one or more persons *engage* with others in such a way that leaders and followers raise one another to higher levels of motivation and morality" (p. 20). They do this, as Bennis and Nanus (1985) explained, by "developing a vision for the organization, developing commitments and trust among workers, and facilitating organizational learning" (p. 403). Through their dispositions and corresponding behaviors, Bass (1985) added, transforming leaders

> convert followers to disciples; they develop followers into leaders. They elevate the concerns of followers on Maslow's (1954) need hierarchy from needs for safety and security to needs for achievement and self-actualization, increase their awareness and consciousness of what is really important, and move them to go beyond their own self-interest for the good of the larger entities to which they belong. The transforming leader provides followers with a cause around which they can rally. (p. 467)

In contrast to Burns's (1978) original view, Bass claimed that transformational leadership does not substitute for transactional leadership, appealing mostly to rational processes and individual self-interest. He suggested that the best leaders are both transformational and transactional, arguing that transformational approaches can augment the effects of transactional behaviors. In any case, the role of leader, from a transformational perspective, is to help make events meaningful for colleagues (Yukl, 1989). Chapters 7 and 8 offer a more detailed account of those transformational school leadership practices that make powerful positive contributions to the emotional lives of teachers.

More About the Book's Purpose

A significant slice of the educational literature concerned with teacher emotions seems primarily to serve the purpose of heightening our understanding and appreciation of the inevitably emotional nature of teachers' work: teachers' anger at wrong-headed district initiatives, frustration with parents who ignore the school's expectations of their children, the joys and satisfactions that come with signs of students' understanding, and the increased sense of efficacy resulting from sharing practices with other teachers. All of these feelings are considered, within this literature, as prima facie evidence that teaching is complex, intense, interpersonal work. Such feelings, according to much of this literature, need to be acknowledged for us to appreciate better what it is like to teach and to respect the work of teachers appropriately. It is not trivial work that they do, nor is it work very well captured by the language of technique or behavior, although teaching clearly entails both. As Hargreaves (1998) eloquently explained,

> Good teaching is charged with positive emotion. It is not just a matter of knowing one's subject, being efficient, having the correct competences or learning all the right techniques. Good teachers are not just well-oiled machines. They are emotional, passionate beings who connect with their students and fill their work and their classes with pleasure, creativity, challenge and joy. (p. 835)

Without doubt, knowing something of the psychological costs to teachers of doing their jobs well sets the stage for addressing such issues as teacher well-being and turnover. Some of this literature considers teaching as emotional work and offers sensible "implications" for the improvement of practice (e.g., Hargreaves, 2001). But very little of it has directly tested such implications to see how they actually matter.

While we believe the "appreciative" purpose served by this type of research on teacher emotions to be worthy, that purpose is not ours. Our goals are decidedly more instrumental. Expanding on our initial formulation of purposes, we take the understanding of teaching as an emotionally intense form of work as the starting point for exploring empirical evidence about what this means for teachers' school and classroom practices and the impact those emotions and practices, together, are known to have on student learning. Our objective for the book is to clarify how those providing leadership in schools can help nurture and maintain positive emotions among individual teachers and a positive emotional climate across the school as a whole. And part of this involves moving into admittedly uncomfortable territory—reflectively and respectfully—alone and with others. Evidence described in subsequent chapters suggests that few leadership initiatives are likely to contribute more to school reform and the improvement of student learning.

In their comprehensive and highly regarded text *Understanding Emotions*, Oatley, Keltner, and Jenkins (2006) offered what is, to our minds, a compelling explanation for the effects of teacher emotions on their school and classroom practices:

> Emotions have principled, systematic effects upon cognitive processes and . . . lead to reasonable judgements about the world. . . . Emotions structure perception, direct attention, give preferential access to certain memories and bias judgment in ways that help the individual to respond to the environment in ways that we recognize as valuable aspects of our humanity. (p. 260)

Emotions act as heuristics, educated guesses, or shortcuts to decision making and to moral judgments when, as is often the case, we have less than complete information with which to make a decision, as of course is almost always the situation faced by teachers in their moment-to-moment interactions with students. Emotions, as we have learned from recent brain research (Damasio, 1997), are inseparable from thought. Positive emotions, furthermore, enhance access to one's existing knowledge, imagination, and creativity; whereas negative emotions can constrain one's thinking and reduce one's ability to access one's store of knowledge and skill in a flexible manner. Positive emotions are associated with optimism and hope for the future.

In a nutshell, then, emotions guide our thinking in ways that allow us to act "sensibly" under conditions of uncertainty. On these grounds, it is hard to imagine a profession more dependent on emotions to guide action than the teaching profession. So understanding teacher emotions would seem to be at the heart of understanding why teachers act as they do. Understanding how to assist teachers in maintaining positive emotional states would seem to be a central understanding for successful school leadership.

Our Evidence

We draw most heavily on four sources of evidence in support of our claims throughout the book. One source is an extensive review of empirical literature on teachers' working conditions originally undertaken for Ontario's elementary teachers' association (Leithwood, 2005). This review included a large sample of original empirical studies (91), supplemented with systematic reviews of relevant evidence (26) published in reputable refereed journals. In addition, the review included a half-dozen recent working conditions and teacher turnover studies conducted by or for teacher federations or unions. This evidence is used to justify most of the claims in Chapters 2 through 6, and the number of studies relevant to each emotion is noted in the section describing each emotion.

Chapters 7 through 9 draw on a longstanding program of transformational school leadership research (e.g., Leithwood & Jantzi, 2005, 2006; Leithwood, Jantzi, & Steinbach, 1999), significantly extended by evidence from research in Ontario on teacher emotions (e.g., Hargreaves, Beatty, James-Wilson, Lasky, & Schmidt, in press) and evidence from England, Ireland, Canada, US, New Zealand, and Australia about the emotions of leaders (Beatty, 2002, 2005, 2006).

Finally, the words of teachers and leaders used to illustrate our claims throughout the book come from transcripts of interviews with a large sample of American teachers and administrators, collected as part of a larger study of leadership effects (Leithwood, Louis, Anderson, & Wahlstrom, 2004) along with Beatty's research, cited above. To be clear, these quotes are introduced not as evidence of our claims but as rhetorical devices to clarify the meaning of our claims.

Framing the Book

Our thinking about the book and its organization was influenced by a simple working "theory" about how all the pieces we address in the book fit together. To begin, we take as our premise that what people do depends on what they think *and* feel—their "internal states." No matter the job or person, the material, social, cultural, and technical conditions of work influence a very large proportion of peoples' overt actions, depending, it should be stressed, on their perceptions and reactions to those conditions. Such perceptions and reactions include, for example, the sense people make of their working conditions, the purposes they believe their working conditions are designed to serve (e.g., educational or political), how they feel about them, what they believe about their source (e.g., whether it is credible or not), and the motives they attribute to those responsible for their working conditions (e.g., student welfare or narrow self-interest).

As Figure 1.1 suggests, teachers' feelings and knowledge (internal states) are the immediate "causes" of what teachers do in their classrooms and schools. Our book is concerned with feelings or emotions, which are closely bound to the more cognitive states— knowledge and skills—involved in acquiring the knowledge and skills that mostly preoccupy school reform efforts. The evidence underpinning Chapters 2 through 6 points to the influence on teachers' practices and student learning of five clusters of emotion, each of which is awarded its own chapter: job satisfaction and morale; stress, anxiety, and burnout; individual and collective self-efficacy; organizational commitment and engagement; and, finally, motivation to change.

Our chapter-length discussion of each cluster of emotions includes a synopsis of the evidence on which the discussion is based and a description of how the cluster of emotions is defined or conceptualized. Each chapter also reviews evidence about the effects of that cluster of emotions on teachers' performance and/or student learning and identifies the leadership practices and other working conditions known to influence those emotions.

The five clusters of emotions are significantly and quite directly influenced by school leadership and working conditions that teachers experience. Of course, working conditions in the school are not the whole story. As Day and his colleagues (2006) have demonstrated quite conclusively, for example, much of the tension, anxiety, and frustration—not to mention commitment—that teachers experience arise from their efforts to balance the conditions of their work with the demands of their private lives and their personal career trajectories. Furthermore, some of the causes of teacher emotions include personal traits, such as teachers' locus of control, or demographic characteristics, such as teachers' age, experience, and education. We do not, however, award influences of this sort much attention, because the majority of evidence indicates that teachers' inside-the-school experiences typically outweigh, or "wash out," the effects of personal and demographic variables on their emotions.

Figure 1.1 also identifies four consequences of teachers' emotions and other internal states:

- *Teachers' classroom practices or performance.* This includes everything a teacher does in the classroom environment to manage the behavior of students (e.g., establishing routines and expectations, designing the physical space, and responding

Figure 1.1

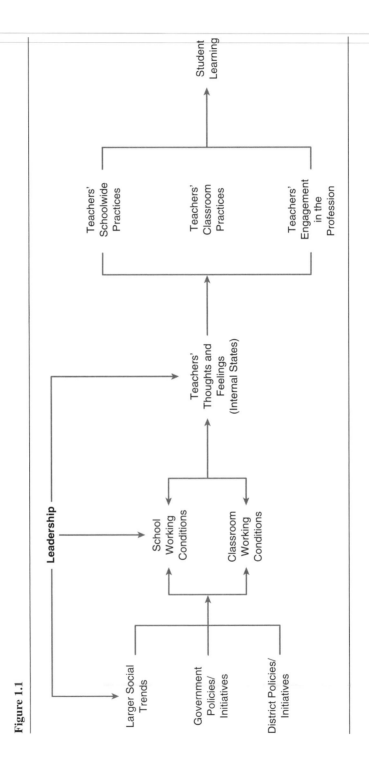

to "situations" on a moment-to-moment basis) and to foster their learning (e.g., scheduling the use of time, planning and delivering instruction, providing suitable learning materials, monitoring student learning, and providing feedback to students and parents).

- *Teachers' schoolwide practices or performance.* This encompasses the many professional activities outside their classrooms needed to maintain the school's organization and to ensure that the school experiences of students are coherent and productive. Teachers, for example, may collaborate with one another in the planning of instruction; act as members of school improvement planning teams and school councils; provide advice to administrators on a wide range of issues; and, frequently, both lead and staff the cocurricular program of the school.

- *Teachers' engagement in the profession.* This includes teachers' intentions and actual decisions and actions relative to continuing in their current school, moving to another school, or quitting the profession altogether. Attention to this outcome is justified by the longstanding, and recently quite urgent, concern about teacher shortages and turnover.

- *Student learning.* However narrowly or broadly conceived and measured, this goes along with students' attitudes toward school and their own learning.

Finally, as Figure 1.1 suggests, the efforts or behaviors of those providing leadership are among the most powerful direct sources of influence on teachers' working conditions and both direct and indirect sources of influence on teacher emotions.

CHAPTER TWO

Looking Forward to Work

Job Satisfaction and Morale

> I can't believe they pay me to do this stuff because it's really fun . . . I just really think it's fun to be a teacher. . . . I had no idea what I wanted to do in college. I just went to college. And then, just really discovered teaching. The students are great. I just like the students a lot. And I think our staff is really fun, too. We're . . . a young staff. And I think our administrators are really supportive . . . they never settle for something that's good. They only want the best. And they want the best out of you. (fifth-grade teacher)

Now *that's* job satisfaction! Who knew it could be so good! Satisfaction and morale are closely related emotions. Sometimes they are treated as overlapping feelings, but much of the empirical research examines them as separate sets of feelings. Job satisfaction captures overall feelings about one's work in the present, while morale is a more future-oriented feeling. Together, they add up to the general disposition teachers have toward their work—whether another day at school is something to look forward to with anticipation if not eagerness, or it's just another day to get through.

JOB SATISFACTION

The amount of evidence concerning job satisfaction in many different sectors, including education, is both large and mature. The treatment of it in this chapter is based on a dozen empirical studies[2] published between 1998 and 2004, along with five reviews, the oldest published in 1976 (Locke), the most recent in 1991 (Schnake). None of the reviews specifically focused on the job satisfaction of teachers, whereas all but one of the original studies focused on teachers. It is worth noting, however, that most factors influencing job satisfaction are much the same across sectors; much can be learned about the causes and consequences of teacher job satisfaction from research conducted in nonschool contexts.

What Is It?

Job satisfaction has been defined as "a pleasurable or positive emotional state resulting from the appraisal of one's job or job experiences" (Locke, 1976, p. 1300); "a state of mind determined by the individual's anticipation of the extent of satisfaction of those needs which s/he perceives as significantly affecting his/her work situation" (Evans, cited in Rhodes, Nevill, & Allan, 2004, p. 68); and the "degree to which an employee has positive emotions toward work" (Currivan, 2000, p. 497). As these definitions imply, job satisfaction is often viewed as a global feeling, as in this chapter. But some research has explored more specific sources or forms of satisfaction, including intrinsic sources, supervision, coworkers, promotion, pay, and the work itself (Mathieu & Zajac, 1990).

Motivation (taken up in more depth in Chapter 6) and job satisfaction are related concepts. But Miskel and Ogawa (1988), arguing for the importance of distinguishing between them, suggested that motivation is a direct cause of behavior, whereas job satisfaction is not. For example, most teachers would experience a sense of satisfaction when a student, struggling to understand rational numbers, finally seems to "get it." But something more than this experience of

---

2. Recall from Chapter 1 that Chapters 2 through 6 are largely based on a total of 91 original studies and 26 reviews. The 12 original studies of job satisfaction were among the 91 in total. Comparable information is provided as part of the treatment of all other emotions in Chapters 2 through 6.

satisfaction is required before most teachers would decide to address the challenges and the personal costs associated with implementing a new program intended to help all of their students "get it." Viewed in this light, satisfaction is a pleasant feeling likely to reinforce one's existing practices and contribute, along with other feelings, to the likelihood of sustaining those practices. This sense of job satisfaction is illustrated in a comment made by a junior high teacher whom we interviewed:

> This is a wonderful place to work. The kids are really good kids. They try to be bad, but they are good kids. We have a lot of excellent teachers on staff who really care about what happens to their students.

Motivation, in contrast, is a more intense feeling likely to produce some action, some change in one's existing practices.

Why Does It Matter?

For many years, research in different organizational contexts portrayed the relationship between job satisfaction and organizational performance—student learning, in the case of schools—as weak (Locke, 1976). But this portrayal typically resulted from studies that viewed satisfaction and performance as individual-level variables. More recent evidence examining these relationships at the organizational level have found much stronger relationships. Ostroff's (1992) study, for example, carried out with a large sample of teachers in junior high and secondary schools, found job satisfaction to be the best predictor of student achievement among all the attitudinal variables measured (i.e., organizational commitment, adjustment to the school, and stress). Considerable evidence indicates that job satisfaction has a strong direct effect on teacher retention (e.g., Stockard & Lehman, 2004), consistent with the sustaining effects of satisfaction we described above.

Ostroff's (1992) study also found a strong relationship between teachers' lack of job satisfaction and their intention to quit the profession. This finding echoes a significant body of research conducted in both school and nonschool settings about the relationships between job satisfaction, organizational commitment, and both the intent to leave the job and the actual behavior of leaving. While this research is reviewed in more detail in Chapter 5, it is worth noting here that the effect of satisfaction on decisions to remain in or leave the organization or profession are significant (e.g., Ingersoll, 2001a, 2001b), although often considered to operate largely indirectly through organizational commitment.

Another line of research conducted mostly in nonschool contexts (e.g., Batemen & Organ, 1983; Organ, 1990; Schnake, 1991) suggests that job satisfaction arising from employees' conceptions of fairness in the "exchange relationship" (the range of rewards provided for work) with their organizations, as well as generally positive feelings about their work, is significantly associated with spontaneous, voluntary actions termed organizational citizenship behaviors (OCB), which are explained more fully below. This sense of fairness, or the lack of it, can arise from many sources, as these remarks from a third-grade teacher we interviewed indicate:

> We're finding that the aides get better treatment than we do. And so do the secretaries. When the aides go to recess, they come back and get a 15-minute break. Teachers who go to the recess may not get a bathroom break all morning, or most of the afternoon. Come on, folks! Or you go to the bathroom and leave your kids unsupervised . . . that's the way you want it, that's the way it goes . . . We've just had clashes [laughs]. And if you have an opinion, it's not encouraged.

Although not formally prescribed in a job description or an employment contract, discretionary OCBs are highly desirable, if not essential, for the effective functioning of almost all organizations (e.g., Organ, 1990). General examples of OCBs include helping a colleague who is falling behind in the job, being cooperative with administrators, contributing to a positive emotional tone in the workplace, and not wasting time.

The organizational citizenship behavior of teachers, more particularly, consists of their engagement in school-level decision making and other work outside of the classroom not formally written into their job contract. In most schools, such work (and the need for it) is ubiquitous, possibly including assuming the personal cost of ensuring adequate instructional resources in the classroom when the school budget is tight, volunteering to oversee the holiday play, and spending extra time with an especially needy student before and after school each day. These examples are just the tip of the iceberg.

For school leaders, teachers' willingness to do such work is a huge issue. When teachers insist on working only according to contract or being paid for any out-of-classroom work, it becomes almost impossible to maintain the quality of curriculum required to meet the high academic standards now commonly required for almost all students. It also becomes close to impossible to provide the range of cocurricular opportunities so necessary and beneficial to the retention and engagement of many students.

Two explanations are commonly offered for the contribution of job satisfaction to organizational citizenship behavior. One explanation is that the types of prosocial behaviors represented by OCBs are more likely when people experience positive emotions. A second explanation, one with significant implications for those in formal school leader positions, is that when people experience satisfying conditions in their workplaces, many will attempt to reciprocate with those they perceive responsible for those conditions. In this kind of "quid pro quo" explanation, for example, a teacher who believes his principal is going out of her way to provide adequate teaching resources, planning time, and appreciation for a job well done considers it only fair to cooperate with schoolwide initiatives the principal believes to be important for the school.

What Can Leaders Do About It?

School leaders have considerable influence on teachers' job satisfaction. This influence consists not only of the face-to-face behaviors experienced by teachers but also of leaders' efforts that deliberately or inadvertently contribute to teachers' working conditions. Among the most useful sources of evidence about working conditions that contribute to teacher job satisfaction is a series of coordinated international studies carried out with both elementary and secondary teachers by Dinham and his colleagues (Dinham & Scott, 1998, 2000). Conducted by teams in Australia, New Zealand, and England, results of these studies challenged the prevailing "two-factor" theory of teacher satisfaction originating in research by Herzberg, Mausner, and Snyderman (1959) with engineers and accountants and by Sergiovanni (1967) with teachers.

The two-factor theory proposed a mutually exclusive set of job satisfiers and dissatisfiers, job satisfiers or motivators contained in the work itself (mostly what happens in the classroom) and job dissatisfiers attributed to broader working conditions in the school (e.g., interpersonal relations with peers, supervisory practices, and school policies). Dinham and Scott (1998, 2000) challenged the mutually exclusive positioning of satisfiers and dissatisfiers; getting rid of a dissatisfier increased job satisfaction, they found. Of greater practical importance for present purposes, however, Dinham and his colleagues also identified a set of satisfiers outside of the school context entirely. They termed this a "third, outer domain of teacher satisfaction" (2000, p. 379). Their evidence suggested the following:

- Conditions in the classroom, under the teacher's control, were generally associated with job satisfaction (e.g., the intrinsic rewards of teaching—working with students, seeing them achieve, and increasing one's own professional abilities).
- Conditions in the wider social and government sphere (their third domain) generally had a negative effect on teachers' job satisfaction. These conditions included society's views of teachers and their status and government efforts to control and shape education, including the pace of educational change, its management, and related issues of workload (more on this in Chapter 6).
- Conditions in the school (e.g., leadership, decision making, school climate, communication, resources, and local reputation of the school) had the potential either to enhance or diminish teachers' job satisfaction, depending on their nature. One of our third-grade teacher interviewees, faced with a principal whom she believed was incompetent, described her coping as "you just survive and just wait them out."

In all three countries in which this series of studies by Dinham and Scott (1998, 2000) was carried out, variation in workload was the aspect of teaching most strongly associated with overall levels of teacher job satisfaction. The widespread sense among teachers that everyone's workload is excessive is exemplified in these remarks by a fifth-grade teacher whom we interviewed:

> *We need more administrators. We need more leaders here. It'd just be nice if ... it's almost I feel like everyone has too much to do. It's just overwhelming. It's like nobody can possibly do it all. So there are some gaps. And I think everyone's just stretched really thin. Very, very thin. I think we would all like more time to collaborate. I would like more feedback. I'd like to be observed more. But there's just so much time in a day and so much people can do.*

Differences across countries also indicated that the context of teachers' work (new policies and practices introduced from those external to the school) have a significant impact on job satisfaction, a finding consistent with Poppleton, Gershunsky, and Pullin's (1994) results, as well.

Evidence from a sample of five relatively recent studies illustrates the support available for Dinham and Scott's (1998) claims about the potential contribution to teacher job satisfaction—either positive or negative—of school-level conditions (e.g., school climate and supervision practices). Stockard and Lehman (2004) used data from the 1993–1995 nationwide *Schools and Staffing Survey* along with the *Teacher Follow-Up Survey* and some additional survey data in one state, conducted by the National Center for Education Statistics, U.S. Department of Education. Results of their study indicated that lower levels of satisfaction were associated with the following: more challenging classes of students, teaching assignments outside one's area of certification, and inadequate supplies. But the effects of these dissatisfiers diminished considerably when conditions in the school included supportive relationships with teaching colleagues, effective and supportive principals, opportunities to influence decisions about school policy, and control over classroom decisions.

In addition to large-scale survey results that provide a broad brush for discerning patterns among teachers, questions of satisfaction and morale go to notions of the individual self. Several remarkable studies provide insight into teachers as whole persons. Nias drew her inferences from two long interviews that occurred at 10-year intervals with primary teachers and offer insights about primary teachers' core or substantial and situated selves, teachers being "persistently self-referential" (1989, p. 207). This approach helped to distinguish teaching work from other craft occupations. She argued that teachers' satisfaction and motivation are affected by contextual frustrations, which she considers in some depth using Herzberg et al.'s (1959) motivation-hygiene theory. Herzberg's early study of engineers and accountants helped to distinguish environmental factors from internal motivators. He posited two unipolar constructs, which he termed "hygiene factors"—such as light, wages, resources, and interpersonal relationships—and "motivating factors"—such as the work itself, professional growth opportunities, and additional responsibilities. When hygiene factors are problematic, they can cause dissatisfaction. But even when improved, they are not especially motivating. Sources of motivation remain intrinsic to the work itself when there are opportunities for self-actualization (Herzberg et al., 1959).

As with Dinham and Scott (1998), Nias found that instead of hygiene and motivator factors being independent of each other, the opposite was true. Teachers who were frustrated with lack of organization by administrators, unrepaired audiovisual equipment, and interference with their classes became dissatisfied. Nias surmised that the ability of these hygiene factors to interfere with teachers' motivation and job satisfaction stemmed from their role in compromising the core self, which was strongly identified with success at work. The dependence of teachers' motivation and satisfaction on their surroundings led Nias to challenge the applicability of Herzberg's account to primary school teachers.

Beatty's (2000b) subsequent research also called Herzberg's account into question with secondary teachers. In Beatty's study, teachers reported being dissatisfied by leaders' and other interference with their access to the intrinsic satisfaction of their work with students. An additional factor in that study holds relevance to the Nias findings. A group of teachers shared their reflections and helped each other retain their motivation and morale during the early stages of deeply disruptive educational reforms in Ontario and in the local context of problematic administrative relationships. Their "professional family" had the power to offset the effects of frustrating and depressing hygiene factors. The emotional support received within the study group allowed teachers to retain their professional self-confidence and renew their enthusiasm for the profession.

Nias dealt with the issue of teacher-specific responses to hygiene and satisfier conditions by creating a third category of motivators—nonsatisfiers. Beatty went further to suggest that some factors that are considered hygiene factors for people in other professions may reduce teacher motivation when they interfere with their source of intrinsic satisfaction—the rewards of the work with students. Nias considered all hygiene factors as capable of disturbing teacher satisfaction and motivation, demonstrating the importance of context for teacher motivation. Like Beatty, she also noted the importance that teachers attach to being able to talk with others, negotiate shared meanings, and forge a common language. This common language promotes openness to further communication and relationships. In the Nias study, these kinds of conversations provided "sympathy and understanding; giving support; helping the process of reflection upon, and learning from experience . . . [which] enabled individuals to seek and find, through interaction with others, confirmation of their selves" (1989, pp. 207–208).

Huberman (1993), Nias (1989), and Beatty (2000b) all concluded from their research that shared reflection is important and deserves greater attention within school systems. Guided by something called "job enhancement theory" (Hackman & Oldham, 1975), Crow and Pounder (1997) and Pounder (1999) also reported evidence of significantly greater satisfaction for teachers working in teams than for those working in isolation.

Rhodes and colleagues (2004) reported the responses of 368 English primary and secondary teachers to 40 factors potentially influencing their job satisfaction. Among the eight factors below identified by at least 90% of respondents as "deeply satisfying," six (listed first) were school-level factors, all of which can be influenced by emotionally sensitive leaders:

- Working with others to achieve a shared goal
- Friendliness of other staff
- Sharing experiences with one another
- The school's working hard to make learning more effective
- The school's valuing contributions by its members
- A climate of achievement in the school
- Classrooms that stimulate pupil learning
- Classrooms with an atmosphere conducive to learning

All three factors claimed to be "deeply" dissatisfying by at least 90% of respondents were school-level factors, including

- The impact of a new performance management policy
- Society's view of teachers
- Proportion of time spent on administration

Finally, in his survey of a nationally representative sample of U.S. teachers, Ingersoll (2001a, 2001b) found teacher dissatisfaction to be among the primary reasons teachers leave the profession (the others were retirement, school staffing action, personal issues, and alternative employment); about a quarter of all public school teachers in his sample identified dissatisfaction as a reason for turnover. Among the seven causes of dissatisfaction for those who stayed in the profession but changed schools, six were clearly school-level conditions, and the remaining two could be ameliorated in part through school-level action. In order of strength, the seven conditions were as follows:

- Poor salary (47% of respondents to the survey)
- Inadequate administrative support (38%)
- Student discipline problems (18%)
- Lack of faculty influence (13%)
- Lack of community support (12%)
- Unsafe environment (11%)
- Lack of student motivation (10%)

Ten percent of teachers in the Ingersoll studies also believed that inadequate time to prepare was an important source of dissatisfaction. But these results seem to dramatically underestimate the importance of this variable, if recent evidence from Newfoundland and Labrador teachers is any indication. Dibbon (2004) found that adequate preparation time was the strongest predictor of job satisfaction among the 681 teachers in his sample. Planning time is associated with opportunities to reflect, revise, collaborate with peers, and, thus, improve practices over time. These are all dimensions that are associated with the intrinsic satisfaction of the work itself, and all are constrained by a lack of planning time.

Results of these studies are generally consistent with Dinham and Scott's (1998, 2000) claim that school-level working conditions can serve either to enhance or diminish teachers' job satisfaction. In addition, however, school-level working conditions appear, based on these studies, to be especially powerful sources of satisfaction. This finding is noteworthy, because many of these conditions are highly improvable with the intervention of effective leadership.

Evidence about teachers' job satisfaction identifies many conditions in the classroom and school with the potential to erode such satisfaction. A recent study of teachers in Prince Edward Island, for example, found significant differences in job satisfaction between teachers with classes ranging from 16 to 30 students as compared with teachers whose classes exceeded 30 students (Belliveau, Liu, & Murphy, 2002).

In spite of this fairly gloomy evidence, Matsui and Lang Research (2005) recently reported that, although Ontario elementary teachers generally felt overworked, stressed, and not hopeful about their working conditions improving any time soon, almost all "were either very or somewhat satisfied with their current teaching position" (p. iv)! This evidence suggests that the intrinsic satisfactions that come from helping children learn, while not alone, dominate the factors influencing teachers' job satisfaction. What leaders can do about all of this is see that access to the factors that improve teacher satisfaction with their classroom teaching experiences are optimized and factors that detract are reduced.

MORALE

This discussion about morale is based on evidence from three reviews of research and seven empirical studies. Two of the reviews were carried out in education contexts (Black, 2001; Lumsden, 1998) and one in a noneducation context (Locke, 1976). The original studies were published between 1991 and 2002.

What Is It?

Common uses of the term *morale* suggest that it is a generalized and relatively enduring state of mind. Good morale is typically associated with hopeful attitudes, an optimistic view toward one's colleagues, and enthusiasm for one's work, whereas poor morale is associated with cynicism, feelings of despair, and lack of enthusiasm.

Conceptions of morale used by researchers largely reflect this common usage. For example, Reyes and Imber (1992) considered morale to be "an employee's attitude toward working conditions, on-the-job services, personnel policies, and relationships with superordinates" (p. 293). Evans (1997) defined it as "a state of mind determined by the individual's anticipation of the extent of satisfaction of those needs which s/he perceives as significantly affecting her/his total work situation" (p. 832). Locke (1976) considered morale to be "an attitude of satisfaction with, desire to continue in, and willingness to strive for the goals of a particular group or organization" (p. 1300). Morale is "the feeling a worker has about his job based on how the worker perceives himself in the organization and the extent to which the organization is viewed as meeting the worker's needs and expectations" (Washington & Watson, cited in Lumsden, 1998, p. 2). As one of seven features of a "healthy" school, Hoy, Tartar, and Witkoskie (1992) considered morale to be "the sense of trust, confidence, enthusiasm and friendliness among teachers" (p. 183). This conception of morale is reflected in the description of her school provided by this third-grade teacher:

> We have a great professional staff. We have a great team of teachers in our building that work hard to do what's best for kids and are dedicated. They're here early, they're here late, they take work home with them. We're an extremely dedicated staff. And a friendly and good group to work with. . . . This is a good building to work in. It really is. . . . Teachers in this particular school have spent most of their careers in this one school. They love the school; they like the community; they felt comfortable. It is a cohesive staff. They believe in what they are doing.

Morale and job satisfaction are usually considered to be different but interdependent states of mind. Morale is more future oriented and anticipatory, whereas job satisfaction is present oriented and a response to some current set of circumstances. A person who achieves job goals or believes progress is being made toward them should feel more confident about the future than someone who is not so successful.

Why Does It Matter?

Teacher morale is associated with a number of teacher behaviors as well as student achievement. Zigarelli (1996) used three sets of data taken from the *National Educational Longitudinal Study* by the National Center for Education Statistics, U.S. Department of Education, to test the effects on student achievement of a small set of often-identified characteristics of effective schools. Contrary to the focus of so much attention over the past 20 years, he found little support for most of those widely touted characteristics. But high teacher morale was strongly associated with student achievement. Others have reported similar results (e.g., Black, 2001).

Examples of teacher behaviors associated with poor morale include less effective teaching performance (Reyes & Imber, 1992), teacher absenteeism (Briggs & Richardson, 1992), and resistance to change (Briggs & Richardson, 1992) because of its negative effect on attitudes, self-esteem, and self-concept. Poor morale also has been associated with teacher turnover (Rafferty, 2002).

What Can Leaders Do About It?

Some evidence suggests that working conditions may have different effects on teacher morale and other emotions depending on teachers' years of experience. Beginning teachers, in particular, have fewer resources to fall back on if they find themselves in less than ideal circumstances, as they often do. These comments by one of our Grade-8 interviewees, a first-year teacher, illustrate such vulnerability:

> There's a total lack of continuity within the language arts department in this school. And I'm not sure that's negative. It just kind of is what it is. We're all three, the three eighth-grade teachers, very different personality styles. And all are pretty capable and pretty alike. I like my style and I like what I do. Having said that, I realize I don't care how capable I am, I'm still a first-year teacher. I still would love help and direction and those things. But unless it's really formally asked for, my colleagues are not going to seek me out to help me. I don't know where that is in a job description— "help out young teachers." But I really was counting on it this year, and really didn't have it, so there was a lot of guessing and checking and kind of like, "Wow, that failed; okay let's try something else." Whereas now I feel pretty solid in the path I've taken, I wouldn't say any of that came from other language arts teachers or administrators.

This recognition of a new teacher's vulnerability accounts for the focus on beginning teachers by Weiss (1999). Her study used data collected by the U.S. Department of Education through its

Schools and Staffing Survey administered in both 1997–1998 and 1993–1994. A total of 5,088 beginning teachers responded to these two surveys.

Results of this study found that the same working conditions influenced not only beginning teachers' morale but their career choice, commitment, and plans to remain or leave teaching as well. Teachers' perceptions of these working conditions outweighed other factors considered in the study, including teachers' demographic characteristics (e.g., age), academic background, and salary. These influential working conditions included

- *School leadership.* Good beginning teachers' morale was associated with support and encouragement from principals. Such leadership included clear communication of expectations, provision of instructional guidance and resources, recognition of good work, and enforcement of student rules of conduct.
- *Student behavior/social climate.* The morale of beginning teachers was significantly influenced by the nature and range of student problems encountered in their classes. Unsafe and disruptive school climates, including tardiness, misbehavior, and physical threats from students, contributed to low morale.
- *Teacher autonomy and discretion.* First-year teachers who experienced autonomy and discretion had significant control over decisions about curricula, texts, forms of instruction, and disciplinary methods. Such discretion stimulated professional learning and fostered an internalized sense of responsibility and accountability for student learning.

Working conditions associated with teacher morale in Weiss's study of beginning teachers have also been reported in studies with more experienced teachers. In addition, positive teacher morale has been associated with teachers' perceptions of the fairness of their workloads (Reyes & Imber, 1992) and opportunities for ongoing professional development (Baylor & Ritchie, 2002). Indeed, teachers' lives have been studied as a progression of stages. Huberman (1993), employing the paradigm of the personal life cycle, observed teachers' emphases on different kinds of concerns and anxieties in the early, middle, and later years of their careers. Early-career teachers needed feedback and guidance, middle-career teachers appreciated more independence, and later-career teachers appreciated sharing their expertise. Both middle- and late-career teachers sought empowerment and collaboration with their leaders. There is clear guidance for leaders in this study; it points to the value of differential and deferential treatment of teachers according to their career stages.

Based on both qualitative and quantitative evidence collected from teachers in Israeli elementary and secondary schools, Nir (2002) reported a negative effect on teachers' morale of the implementation of school-based management (SBM) practices. A sharp drop in teacher morale occurred in the second year of implementation, apparently due to increased internal pressures for accountability and the struggle for resources among teachers. These challenges were likely to have been, as Nir explains, significantly at odds with what teachers expected to happen as SBM was implemented.

Blase and Anderson's (1995) study is described at some length here because of its especially valuable insights about the influence of leaders' practices on teacher emotions, including morale. In this study, the nature of the teacher-leader relationship had important consequences for teacher emotions and signaled the relevance of teachers' emotionally based interpretations of what leaders do to their feelings of satisfaction and morale. Leaders' practices were categorized as relatively "open" versus "closed" and "transformative" versus "transactional." Combining these distinctions produced four "styles" of leadership: adversarial (transformative closed), democratic (transformative open), authoritarian (transactional closed), and facilitative (transactional open), each of which is described more fully below. Teachers in facilitative leadership environments experienced such positive emotions as esteem, pride, satisfaction, confidence, security, and inclusion. These teachers were also inclined toward increased involvement, awareness, and reflection. They enjoyed their leaders' honest, constructive, nonthreatening manner and felt that their ability to understand their personal and professional needs was crucial. They valued the willingness of leaders to "engage in 'face-to-face' collaborative decision-making" and to create "relationships with teachers that minimized 'status difference' and promoted teacher autonomy and authority" (Blase & Anderson, 1995, p. 81). Facilitative leaders tended to ask rather than tell, and teachers were free to disagree and say no. Teachers also appreciated these facilitative principals because they were courteous, personable, easygoing, unpressured, and disinclined to get hung up on details and rules.

The importance of leaders' humor and timing also became apparent in this study. Rather than being considered weak, open principals were viewed as maintaining authority in humane and inoffensive ways. Leaders' supportiveness was directly related to their accessibility by teachers. Teachers valued the willingness of these leaders to "stand behind their teachers" in confrontations with students and parents, especially in student discipline contexts. Additionally, teachers felt supported by the facilitative leader's "visibility throughout the school" and provision of information that was "timely and relevant" (Blase & Anderson, 1995, p. 82).

This study points, as well, to the importance of how leaders think of and refer to people who don't agree with them: "Conflict is derailed early on by appealing to bureaucratic discourse. This is done through the common practice of labeling resistant subordinates as, for example, 'negative,' 'not a team player,' 'troublemaker,' and 'emasculating'" (Blase & Anderson, 1995, p. 138). In this way, some leaders fend off criticism by marginalizing and pathologizing the individual "through labeling in order to protect the legitimacy of the institution" (Blase & Anderson, p. 138). This silencing by marginalizing clearly had a damaging effect on the morale of teachers in this study. Influence, association, reciprocation, and mutual benefit were matters of diplomacy, and researchers found these to be "essential to the curricular and extracurricular work performance of teachers" (Blase & Anderson, p. 70). However,

> According to teachers, being diplomatic was related to limiting the expression of negative emotions. Frequently, this meant "biting your tongue . . . and smiling, despite one's feelings. Regardless of the issue, loss of control and/or aggressiveness usually resulted in serious loss of reputation. . . . Teachers tended to avoid or withdraw from those who failed to display composure in their interactions. . . . [and] conformed to norms of conventional politeness. (Blase & Anderson, p. 70)

In Blase and Anderson's study (1995), teachers who revealed their dissent lost power, and when this happened, teachers reported feeling "resentful, hostile, frustrated, disgusted, outraged, bitter, violated, used, exploited"; they also reported feeling "out of control" and "alienated, negative, defeated, sad, humiliated, disheartened and depressed" as well as "confused, disoriented, uncertain, uneasy, fearful, scared, nervous, paranoid and anxious" (pp. 40–41). These emotions were associated with controlling leadership practices. And there were other consequences for teachers:

> An overwhelming portion of the data supports the general conclusion that the use of control tactics by school principals . . . tends to have profound negative consequences for teachers. . . . [This includes] reductions of teacher work time in the classroom and in the school . . . and [decreased] teacher control of decisions, decreases in concern for improvement, and increases in the difficulty of student problems. . . . Fully 71% of the research participants reported negative outcomes for their classroom performance; 80% described negative effects for their school wide performance. (p. 42)

Depictions of teachers' remaining silent for their own survival are characteristic of closed, transactional, authoritarian leadership practices that include censure, favoritism, and overcontrol (Blase & Anderson, 1995). Stasis and demoralization are typical outcomes of leadership that does not allow people to voice their criticisms (Hargreaves, 1998). Such oppressive regimes are unhealthy for teachers and damaging to teacher morale.

CONCLUSION

Evidence reviewed in this chapter places the practices of leaders very near the center of the factors that account for teachers' job satisfaction and morale. These two sets of emotions significantly shape what teachers do in schools and classrooms; they are, as well, pivotal in teachers' decisions about continuing in the profession or looking for other work. The point that emerges quite clearly from this chapter, one that needs to be emphasized, is that the so-called "soft" interpersonal relationships that leaders and teachers build together are likely to be a more potent force in teachers' emotional lives and their views of the teaching profession than such "hard" factors as salaries and even class sizes.

We do not mean to minimize the importance of the "hard" factors. They clearly do make a difference to how teachers feel about their work. But their influence on teacher emotions pales in comparison to the interpersonal relationships between teachers and their leaders. Interpersonally indifferent or hostile relationships will drive teachers away no matter what other working conditions they enjoy, while interpersonally rich and empathetic relationships inure teachers against a host of less-than-perfect working circumstances.

CHAPTER THREE

Wanting to Stay Home

Stress, Anxiety, and Burnout

THELMA'S STORY

Thelma is a math teacher in an urban secondary school serving a high proportion of pretty needy kids, many of whom speak English as their second language. She likes teaching math, and although it was not her college major, she has taken advantage of most of the district and state professional development opportunities that have been offered over her five-year career to improve her knowledge of both math content and pedagogy. She is a very committed teacher. Thelma also has high aspirations for her students, sincerely believing that virtually all of them can succeed in her courses under the right conditions.

But lately Thelma has begun to feel a bit depressed. The idealism she brought to her job just a few short years ago has been seriously challenged in the past year by a confluence of developments that have really been a distraction from her direct work with her students. The administrative paperwork she is now responsible for has escalated dramatically. In spite of her own high aspirations for her students, many of the parents of her students this year seem to hold relatively low expectations for the academic achievement of their children. So she feels she is not getting much support from home.

The school as a whole has experienced a substantial increase in student absenteeism and this has meant spotty attendance for a large handful of students in Thelma's math classes. On top of all this, the new principal is a rookie and seems to feel the need to make all decisions herself. This has resulted in quite a bit of conflict with staff, and some of Thelma's closest colleagues are actively looking for transfers to other schools. While Thelma used to look forward to going to work most days, she has begun to dread it. She is beginning to feel powerless to change a deteriorating set of working conditions and can't see much reason for optimism in the near future.

(to be continued)

Although Thelma's story is a depressing one, it is far from rare. Expectations for student achievement have become increasingly ambitious and accountability for reaching such high standards increasingly public and demanding. Often, it seems, neither policy makers nor members of the public at large have much appreciation for the work of teachers, the challenges they face with increasingly diverse groups of students, or the deteriorating conditions in which a remarkable number of teachers currently work. Media reports about schools are heavily weighted toward criticism.

Now if teachers didn't care much about their work and their students, these challenges and negative conditions might be considered to be just so much "noise." Developing a "thick skin" might be the answer, as might trying a different job altogether. But, as a group, teachers are arguably among the world's most dedicated group of professionals, and committed teachers would prefer to persevere rather than opt out. They feel called to help kids learn. But conditions that prevent teachers from doing their jobs well, along with unfair and often uninformed criticism of their work, hurt a lot. The more committed you are, the more it matters. So an initial state of general anxiety about work easily develops into feelings of stress about specific conditions associated with the job. Work overload, role conflict, and role ambiguity contribute to emotional exhaustion, resulting in depersonalization or detachment from students and a loss of a sense of personal accomplishment (Maslach & Jackson, 1981). These are all factors and outcomes associated with burnout (Dworkin, Saha, & Hill, 2003).

We know quite a bit about anxiety, stress, and burnout and the factors that both ameliorate and give rise to these closely related feelings; leadership behaviors are especially prominent among them. The evidence we draw on in this chapter comes from two reviews of research (Kyriacou, 2001; Leithwood, Menzies, Jantzi, & Leithwood, 1996) and 17 original empirical studies published between 1974 and 2003. Our primary focus will be on burnout, the most negative and consequential of these closely related internal working conditions. Everyone experiences some anxiety about their work from time to time. It is unavoidable. And stress can have both positive and negative consequences. However, the consequences of burnout are uniformly unpleasant for both teachers and their students, and burnout is avoidable.

What Is It?

As you will understand by now, burnout (the term was first introduced by Freudenberger in 1974) manifests itself as an extreme form of stress, one most often experienced by those who work in interpersonally intense occupations, such as nursing, teaching, and the service industries more generally. Those engaging in such occupations are subject to chronic tension (Cunningham, 1983) and often have only weak levels of control over their own work. Teachers, for example, have considerable control over their plans for each day's instruction. But they have very little control over the standards they must meet with their students, the effects of disruptive family events on the readiness to learn of some of their students on any given day, false fire alarms and bomb scares that clear the school in the middle of a tricky science experiment, and, in a great many districts, the selection of their next vice principal.

And those sources of uncertainty for teachers are really just the superficial ones! Your average middle school teacher, for example, faces the task of keeping 30 lively teenagers (bursting with hormones) meaningfully engaged in their academic tasks for an hour or more at a time. While most middle school teachers learn how to manage this fundamental challenge, just think of the possibilities. If that isn't a stress-inducing situation to face all day every day, what is? Most parents have great difficulty retaining the attention of one teenage child for more than 10 minutes at a time.

The term *burnout* signifies the inability of people to function effectively in their jobs as a consequence of prolonged and extensive stress related to those jobs (Byrne, 1991). Stress and burnout are closely related states of mind. Dworkin (1987) argued that the greater the level of stress, the greater the level of burnout. But once burnout has reached a high level, it may actually reduce stress. As Dworkin explained, at that point "burnout becomes a coping mechanism through which teachers cease to care and thereby experience reduced stress" (p. 77).

Maslach and Jackson (1981), authors of a widely used tool for diagnosing burnout, claimed that it is a three-dimensional state of mind including the following:

- *Feelings of emotional exhaustion or wearing out.* Teachers no longer feel able to devote themselves to their students to the same extent as earlier in their careers. Thelma is experiencing the early stages of such exhaustion.
- *Depersonalization.* Teachers develop negative, cynical, and callous attitudes toward students, parents, and their teaching colleagues. If conditions in her school don't begin to change noticeably over the next year, Thelma's early idealism may be permanently extinguished.
- *Reduced sense of personal accomplishment and esteem.* Teachers no longer believe themselves to be effective in helping their students to learn and in accomplishing their other duties, a feeling already plaguing Thelma.

Why Does It Matter?

Burnout has significant negative effects on teachers themselves, their schools, and their students. Teachers suffering from excessive stress or burnout are increasingly absent from the job (*wanting* to stay home escalates into *actually* staying home). Their classroom performance declines; since it seems like such an uphill battle to get the job done well, they cease continuing to try. Relationships with both colleagues and students are eroded. These teachers are less sympathetic toward students and less committed to and involved in their jobs. They have a lower tolerance for classroom disruption, are less apt to prepare adequately for class, and are generally less productive (Blase & Greenfield, 1985; Farber & Miller, 1981). Burned out teachers can have a chilling effect on the morale of new teachers.

Teachers experiencing burnout tend to be more dogmatic about their practices and resist changes to those practices. They are also inclined to treat students in a depersonalized way and resort to victim-blaming for low achievement or failure. Dworkin (1987) summarized evidence indicating that high-achieving students placed with teachers suffering from burnout achieve 20% less, over the course of a year, than do students placed with other teachers. Burnout also is associated with higher rates of student dropout. And while it is strongly associated with the intent to quit teaching, it is only weakly related to actual quitting. Dworkin (1997) proposed that "many burned-out teachers are unable to find work in the private sector that pays comparable salaries, or that does not require substantial retraining" (p. 473).

Teachers do have many skills that are transferable, even if they don't realize it. Unfortunately, though, for most of these teachers and their students, many burned out teachers remain in schools and remain burned out, sometimes for years on end. Estimates of the prevalence of burnout or excessive feelings of stress across the teaching population are actually quite alarming, ranging from 15% to 45% (Dworkin, 1997; Friedman & Farber, 1972; Schlansker, 1987).

What Can Leaders Do About It?

The working conditions of teachers, strongly influenced by those in formal school leader roles, have considerable influence on the extent to which teachers experience anxiety and stress and the frequency with which anxiety and stress escalate into full-blown burnout. To capture what we know about those working conditions, we first present the results of a single, especially comprehensive and well-designed study about these conditions reported by Byrne in 1991. Then we summarize the results of a review of empirical research published by Leithwood and colleagues in 1996, including evidence published before the Byrne study as well as in the subsequent five years. Our analysis of studies published since that time, and there have been quite a few,[3] failed to identify any factors giving rise to teacher stress and burnout beyond those reflected in these two sources.

Key working conditions that either contribute to or help ameliorate burnout among teachers in the Canadian province of Ontario provided the focus of Byrne's 1991 study. Survey data for this study were collected from a total of 423 urban teachers in six elementary

---

3. These studies included Brouwers & Tomic (2000); Chan (2002), Hastings & Bham (2003); Jacobsson, Pousette, & Thylefors (2001); Kyriacou (2001); Moriarty, Edmonds, Blatchford, & Martin, (2001); Rosenblatt (2001); Sava (2002); Tatar & Horenczyk (2003).

schools, six intermediate schools, and four secondary schools. Table 3.1 displays the rankings of the most frequently identified working conditions contributing to burnout for each of these groups of teachers in response to an open-ended question asking them "to list phenomena related to their work which they believed contributed most to feelings of stress" (p. 200). As Byrne indicated, these factors are very similar to the results of earlier research, and there is considerable agreement across the three groups of teachers about the importance of many of the same factors.

Five factors were identified by all three groups, with time constraints clearly the biggest contributor to stress and burnout. A recent Ontario study reported similar results (Matsui & Lang Research, 2005). In order of priority, time constraints is followed by the number of students for which the teacher is responsible, excessive administrative paperwork, lack of support and recognition, and multiple role expectations (e.g., teacher, coach, mentor, and advisor).

Other important contributions to the stress and burnout of elementary teachers were, in order, excessive or unrealistic parental expectations, extracurricular and supervisory duties, the diversity of abilities and needs among students in one's classroom (identified only by elementary teachers), and excessive course loads along with constantly changing curricula to be implemented (also identified only by elementary teachers). Unlike elementary teachers, but hardly surprisingly, intermediate and secondary teachers experienced considerable stress from student discipline, attitude, and behavior issues.

Among elementary teachers, in particular, Byrne's results also indicated that male teachers experienced lower levels of emotional exhaustion than their female colleagues, and teachers in the 40–49 year range experienced higher levels of personal accomplishment than did their younger colleagues.

Tables 3.2 and 3.3 summarize the results of the review of teacher burnout alluded to above (Leithwood et al., 1996). Eighteen empirical studies published between 1984 and 1995 that inquired about both working conditions and, in particular, leadership practices influencing teacher burnout were included in the review. The left column of these tables lists the working conditions; the right column indicates the number of studies, out of a total of 18, that identified each factor as a significant contributor to either increasing or reducing burnout. A substantial number of conditions was identified in only one study.

Table 3.1   Rank Order of Factors Contributing to Teacher Burnout

Factors Contributing to Teacher Burnout	Elementary Teachers	Intermediate Teachers	Secondary Teachers
Excessive administrative paperwork	1	4	8
Time constraints	2	2	1
Number of students	3	1	7
Parent expectations	4	3	
Extracurricular & supervisory duties	5	7	
Variation in students' ability and need	6		
Lack of support and recognition from admin. and parents	7	8	4
Excessive course load; ever-changing curriculum	8		
Multiple role expectations	9	6	10
Student attitudes and behavior		5	2
Student discipline problems		9	9
Apathy and increasing burnout among colleagues		10	5
External personal factors			3
Sense of powerlessness			6

Table 3.2 lists a total of 13 organizational conditions and 13 leadership practices stimulating teachers' feelings of stress and burnout. Among the organizational conditions, most frequently identified was student misbehavior. This is an especially important factor for leaders' attention in the face of evidence from the Organisation for Economic Co-operation and Development's (OECD) recent, massive, multicountry assessment of student achievement and the factors accounting for it. School disciplinary climate was identified in the OECD study as an especially powerful explanation for variation in student achievement across schools (Ma, 2003). A good disciplinary climate is reflected in the sense shared by staff and students alike that maintaining reasonable standards of behavior is everyone's responsibility. School policies are created to reinforce that agreement. Teachers who

Table 3.2   Organizational Conditions and Leadership Practices Contributing to Teacher Anxiety, Stress, and Burnout

Conditions	Number of Studies
Organizational Conditions	
Student misbehavior (discipline, absence, apathy, etc.)	7
Organizational rigidity	3
Hierarchical administrative structures	2
External pressures for change	2
Work overload (excessive paperwork, pupil load)	2
Isolation	2
Overdemand (reduced time for instruction)	1
Underdemand (excessive job prescription)	1
Role conflict and ambiguity	1
Inadequate access to facilities	1
Rigid rules for use of facilities	1
Lack of support	1
Excessive, unrealistic societal expectations	1
Leadership Practices	
Unreasonable expectations of teachers	4
Non-participative/authoritarian leaderships style	3
Inconsistent behavior and expectations	2
Failure to provide adequate instructional resources	2
Lack of follow through	2
Lack of support for staff	2
Excessive emphasis on student achievement	1
Lack of knowledge about teaching and learning	1
Poor teacher evaluation	1
Indecisiveness	1
Favoritism	1
Harassment	1
Lack of trust in teachers' professional capacities	1

Table 3.3   Organizational Conditions and Leadership Practices That
Reduce Teacher Anxiety, Stress, and Burnout

Conditions	Number of Studies
Organizational Conditions	
Support of friends, family, colleagues	7
Having an influence on decisions	5
Opportunities to share professional experiences	1
Recognition leading to advancement	1
Job security	1
Access to support staff	1
Adequate physical facilities	1
Relaxed, flexible use of facilities	1
Flexible administrative structures	1
Reduced workload	1
Opportunities for changing assignments	1
Clear job expectations	1
Leadership Practices	
Generally supportive and considerate	8
Supportive approach to appraisal (recognition, feedback, standards)	5
Participative leadership style	3
Provides emotional support	2
Provides direct assistance when needed	2
Facilitates access to information	1
Modest or balanced emphasis on student achievement	1
Value placed on integration with staff and assisting others	1
High levels of structure (clarity) and consideration	1

identify student misbehavior as a prime cause of burnout are not working in schools with a positive disciplinary climate. More often, they are on their own when it comes to student discipline. Developing a positive disciplinary climate is a very promising contribution to reducing teacher stress and ameliorating the incidence of burnout.

Another organizational condition identified in more than one study was work overload, including pupil load, excessive paperwork, isolation, and organizational rigidity. When the organization constrains how you go about your work (such as by stipulating a highly prescribed use of time, prescriptive curricula, or only one approved instructional technique), you are unable to use your capacities to their fullest; this can feel like trying to get the job done with one hand tied behind your back.

External pressure for change was also a significant condition giving rise to burnout and organizational rigidity in our review of evidence. Of course, schools are regularly bombarded with proposals or mandates for change, some of which may be helpful and many others not so much. If teachers feel the need to respond to all such pressures, they will quickly feel overwhelmed. Leaders are helpful, in the face of such pressure, when they buffer teachers from the feeling that things are constantly changing and assist teachers by acknowledging and ameliorating the emotional and professional impacts of necessary change.

Based on our review of evidence, at least six leadership behaviors or practices appear to exacerbate teacher stress and burnout. One such behavior is unclear or unreasonable expectations on the part of leaders. Teachers are a conscientious group of people overall, and many a teacher has beaten himself up because he felt unable to meet a set of impossible expectations. The Ontario elementary school curriculum has recently been identified as a source of such unreasonable expectations, for example. It contains approximately 3,000 specific expectations or learning goals for students through the end of Grade 8, or roughly 500 per year. In spite of the just plain silliness of such a volume of expectations, many teachers have reported feeling guilty and stressed out about not being able to address them all (see Leithwood, McAdie, Bascia, & Rodrigue, 2004).

Inconsistency is a second leadership behavior contributing to teacher stress. As we shall see later, this doesn't do a thing to build trust among teachers—or administrators. Other leadership behaviors that teachers find stress inducing include a nonparticipative style of leadership, failure to provide essential resources, lack of follow-through on decisions, and lack of acknowledgment and support for the efforts of teachers.

Table 3.3 summarizes organizational conditions and leadership practices that reduce the likelihood of teacher stress and burnout. By far the most frequently identified organizational condition is support from friends, family, and colleagues. For one teacher we interviewed, this support took the form of a well-established personal relationship that made communication easier:

> *When you have a connection with someone off campus, or just a personal connection, it makes it so much easier when you have a problem that comes up to go to that person, because you already have that background with them and that open door of communication.*

Having an influence on decision making in the school and in class was also identified as a stress reducer in multiple studies. This table indicates, as well, that leaders reduce the chances of stress and burnout when they are supportive and considerate and when they use a participative style of decision making in the school.

As we can see from these tables, leaders make a difference in the likelihood of teacher burnout. Within their sphere of influence are the top two organizational conditions: provision of support and the creation of an ethic of openness to being influenced about decisions. Mirroring these organizational conditions are the leadership practices that demonstrate consideration (inferred care) and supportiveness; that provide recognition (inferred respect), feedback, and a shared understanding of workable standards and expectations; and that welcome participation in leadership and decision making. Other leadership practices likely to keep stress at manageable levels include a participative leadership style, direct assistance to teachers when needed (e.g., taking over the teacher's class so the teacher has time to organize an afterschool event), and keeping teachers informed of developments across the school and district. Leaders also help keep teacher stress at a manageable level by adopting a balanced stance toward what counts in school (e.g., emphasis on achievement but acknowledgment of other personal and social goals as well), helping staff align and integrate their efforts, and providing clarity about the school's priorities.

Leaders do influence teachers' inner and outer working conditions. They impact the inner lives of teachers as they create (or overlook) the conditions that speak volumes to teachers about whether they are respected, recognized, considered or cared about, and able to trust they will be professionally and/or personally supported

(Beatty, 2002). The inner world of teachers should be a source of strength and inspiration for their work with students; it is profoundly susceptible to leader influence.

Meanwhile . . .

THELMA'S STORY (CONTINUED)

Three years has elapsed since we first heard about Thelma. It has been something of a roller-coaster ride for her during that time, both personally and professionally. Most of Thelma's close colleagues were successful in transferring out of the school at the end of the year in which we first met Thelma. Because she had difficulty making friends with their replacements and felt that she couldn't consider transferring herself, she was left feeling isolated. She and her husband had decided on a temporary separation, and she didn't want to disrupt the lives of her own children any further; they liked their school and all of their friends went there.

To make matters worse, she found herself struggling to engage the new cohort of students she was assigned and did not know where she could safely turn for help. She wasn't sure the principal could help and worried that her difficulties would be interpreted as a sign of weakness. Her new department head seemed more interested in district committee work than helping his own department colleagues. This further eroded her sense of personal accomplishment, and she began to feel helpless to change things.

By the end of the second year, Thelma, for the first time, was having serious doubts about teaching as a career but didn't know what else she could do and still make a decent salary. She didn't feel nearly as motivated to prepare for class because it didn't seem to matter. Her students were acting out regularly, and she frequently had to call the office for help. She had begun to feel pretty cynical about her students. Thelma was beside herself and seemed to have no one to turn to for help and support.

At this point, Thelma's story could have gone either way. Far too frequently, in the real world, this story has a very unhappy ending. But Thelma got lucky. She happened upon one of her former colleagues by chance (Robin), a person she once considered a best friend at school; they had taken a few car trips together. Robin was shocked at what Thelma unburdened on her and decided to help. Over the summer, Robin and Thelma spent a lot of time together, and for the first time in a long time,

Thelma felt she had someone who understood and cared about her—besides her kids. Along the way, Robin suggested that Thelma confide in her principal. What did she have to lose at this point? And Robin suggested working a bit harder at making connections with some of her recent teacher colleagues. Thelma was reluctant but eventually agreed.

Thelma's third year unfolded more positively. Her principal, as it turns out, was almost completely unaware of Thelma's personal difficulties and not nearly as tuned into her professional difficulties as she now believed she ought to have been. She resolved to help: no extracurricular responsibilities for the year; smaller classes for the first semester until Thelma regains control; more secretarial support for the paperwork; and help in building a coaching/consulting relationship with another teacher on staff, who turned out to have a lot of empathy for what Thelma has gone through, having had similar experiences earlier in her career. Thelma and her principal now touch base every couple of weeks to make sure these changes are helping. They are.

She and her husband decided on a divorce, but by now, life without him doesn't seem so bad.

Thelma's back!

Chapter Four

Persisting Against All Odds

Individual and Collective Self-Efficacy

An extensive body of research has taught us that teachers' beliefs about their abilities can make a world of difference to their actual effectiveness. Over 25 years of research reveals that high levels of teacher self-efficacy are strongly associated with higher levels of student performance. This chapter examines, separately, evidence about the nature and effects of teachers' individual senses of efficacy and the collective efficacy that a group of teachers working together over some time might share. The chapter also describes leadership practices that are well suited to the development of both individual and collective efficacy.

INDIVIDUAL TEACHER SELF-EFFICACY

Evidence about teachers' individual self-efficacy for this chapter was provided by 18 empirical studies published between 1976 and 2006 and five reviews of literature. Four of the five reviews, published over the past decade, summarized evidence collected from teachers only (Goddard & Goddard, 2001; Ross, 1995; Tschannen-Moran & Hoy, 2001; Tschannen-Moran, Woolfolk Hoy, & Hoy, 1998), while one, published some years ago, synthesized evidence about the efficacy of employees primarily in nonschool organizations (Mathiew & Zajac, 1990).

This account of teacher self-efficacy research relies especially heavily on Bandura's (1997) more recent theoretical work and the comprehensive reviews of theory and research by Tschannen-Moran et al. (1998), along with the systematic accumulation of exceptionally high-quality empirical evidence collected through the ongoing program of research of Ross and his colleagues, primarily with elementary teachers (e.g., Ross, 1995; Ross, Hogaboam-Gray, & Hannay, 2001).

What Is It?

Consider this brief excerpt from an interview we conducted with a third-grade teacher in a school serving a high proportion of disadvantaged children:

Interviewer: *You made an observation [earlier] about the shifting socioeconomic [characteristics of your students] that's going on, and there are implications for kids coming to school where they're ready to learn and getting the support from home. Then the school is making up the difference?*

Teacher: *I don't know if we can make up the difference.*

Interviewer: *I was wondering how you felt about that.*

Teacher: *How can we do that? It makes me sad. We started a breakfast program, which is good, because those kids can come in and have breakfast. Some of those kids are here early. Some don't come until late. Sometimes I just shake my head, how can I overcome that? How can I overcome when one little boy got locked out of his house at night because his dad was mad at him? How can I change that? How can I help him learn? I don't know.*

This teacher clearly despairs of overcoming those conditions in her students' family lives that seriously hamper their ability to learn at school. This teacher's projection of her low expectations of the students suggests she has created a negative self-fulfilling prophecy. This is a dangerous and prevalent condition in low socioeconomic status (SES) schools. We will look at a contrasting example a bit later.

The concept of individual teacher efficacy can be traced to the foundational work of Armor and colleagues (1976) and Bandura

(1977). It has been defined as "the extent to which a teacher believes he or she has the capacity to affect student performance" (Berman et al., cited in Tschannen-Moran et al., 1998). It is a belief about one's ability to perform a task or achieve a goal. Such efficacy may be relatively general, as in the teacher's belief about her instructional capacities with all children and all curricula, or more specific, as in the teacher's belief about her ability to teach a specific concept (e.g., evolution) to a specific type of student (e.g., sixth-grade students). To be clear, self-efficacy is a belief about one's ability or capacity, not one's actual ability or capacity; much of self-efficacy theory aims to explain how such beliefs, even when they are inaccurate, eventually produce actual capacities.

Individual self-efficacy beliefs are associated with other thoughts and feelings. For example, Mathieu and Zajac's (1990) "meta-analysis" of research (a summing up of research results in an especially systematic and rigorous way) on organizational commitment in nonschool contexts found strong positive relationships between self-efficacy beliefs, or perceived personal competence, and employees' organizational commitment. Similar results have been found among teachers (Tschannen-Moran et al., 1998). In addition, Parkay, Greenwood, Olejnik, and Proller (1998) found that low levels of teacher self-efficacy have been associated with feelings of stress.

Most research on teachers' sense of self-efficacy has been substantially influenced by the theoretical ideas advanced by Albert Bandura.[4] His theory and research identifies the effects of self-efficacy feelings on teachers' own behavior and the consequences of that behavior for others. This line of theory also specifies the immediate causes or stimulants of self-efficacy beliefs and the mechanisms through which such beliefs develop.

Self-efficacy beliefs shape and influence one's choice of activities and settings and can affect one's efforts to adapt and learn once those activities are begun. Such beliefs determine how much effort teachers will expend and how long they will persist in the face of failure or difficulty. The stronger the self-efficacy, the longer the persistence. For example, faced with a group of ESL students for the first time, Maria has developed considerable confidence in her instructional skills by working in peer coaching relationships and having meaningful and supportive discussions with her principal and other

---

4. For example, see Bandura (1977, 1982, 1986, 1993, 1997).

colleagues about how she is approaching her challenging students. She continues to experiment with new approaches potentially useful to her new students' learning. She is working in an environment within which it is culturally acceptable not to be reticent about calling on other teachers and consultants for help. By the end of the first term, her students are learning well and enjoying Maria's classes.

Sylvia, on the other hand, who began with a very similar group of students, lacks Maria's instructional confidence. She has worked in isolation throughout her career and is insecure about how her work is viewed by others. When Sylvia finds her routine practices are not especially productive for the ESL students, she worries that they, and therefore she, will fail. Not wanting to be viewed as a failure, Sylvia tries even harder to make her well-practiced instructional routines work and masks her anxieties about her difficulties with her colleagues and principal, for fear of being criticized. By the end of the first term, her class is less engaged than ever, falling behind in their progress, and she feels she is losing control of the group. Her self-efficacy at an all time low, Sylvia is now reconsidering her choice of career.

As these stories of Maria and Sylvia illustrate, "Efficacy expectations are a major determinant of peoples' choice of activities, how much effort they will expend and how long they will sustain effort in dealing with stressful situations. . . . Appropriate skills and adequate incentives" (Bandura, 1997, p. 77) are keys to success.

Bandura (1977) has conceptualized self-efficacy along three dimensions: complexity, generality, and strength. When considered in order from simple to complex, peoples' self-efficacy may be limited to relatively simple tasks or extend to the most difficult. Self-efficacy may also be focused on very specific tasks rather than be part of a more generalized view of all of the areas of one's work. For example, Sylvia remains confident of her ability to use phonics to help her new ESL students begin to learn English but remains very uncertain about many of the other tasks she needs to perform. In contrast, self-efficacy may be more broadly conceived as we see with Maria, who is confident about her abilities to instruct virtually any student successfully, no matter the area of curriculum. One also may hold efficacy beliefs weakly or strongly. Maria's instructional efficacy beliefs took quite a lickin'—but kept on tickin'—in the first month of her ESL assignment, whereas Sylvia's tentative beliefs in her instructional capacities were easily snuffed out by the end of her first term with her new ESL students.

Efficacy beliefs, suggested Bandura (1993), develop in response to both cognitive and affective processes. Among the strongest cognitive influences on self-efficacy are beliefs about ability as either "inherent capacity" or "acquired skill." The "inherent capacity" view fosters a concern for protecting one's positive evaluation of one's competence. Teachers holding this view, like Sylvia, are more likely to experience an eroding sense of efficacy as difficulties arise, become more erratic in their problem solving, and lower their aspirations for the individuals or groups in their organization. These lowered aspirations then lead to declines in performance. Maria's "acquirable skills" view, on the other hand, encourages the expansion of her competence. Under this belief system, teachers' own self-judgments change very little in response to challenging circumstances. Teachers like Maria are more likely to continue to set challenging goals for themselves and their colleagues and remain systematic and efficient in their problem solving. This approach is likely to lead to higher levels of organizational performance. Of critical importance for leaders is the recognition that the culture and climate of your school can encourage or discourage the "acquired skill" mind-set (see Rosenholtz & Simpson, 1990).

Also among the cognitive mechanisms influencing efficacy beliefs are perceptions about how controllable or alterable one's working environment relative is for oneself. This perception includes two components: one's ability to influence what goes on in the environment through effort and persistence, and the malleability of the environment itself. Bandura (1993) reported evidence suggesting that those with low levels of belief in how controllable their environment is produce little change even in highly malleable environments (e.g., "I'd like to help these kids more, but I would need much smaller classes to do that."). Those with firm beliefs about their ability to influence their environments, through persistence and ingenuity, figure out ways of exercising some control even in environments with many challenges to change.

Another belief system—locus of control—can have a bearing here (Rotter, 1966; Rotter, 1975; Wang, 1983). Those who feel they have considerable control over their environments are more inclined toward action than passive resignation. Teachers' beliefs about their own efficacy (Ashton & Webb, 1986; Gibson & Dembo, 1984) and locus of control (Wang, 1983) are open to revision through experience. Leaders can engage teachers in experiencing the "acquired skill" belief system through providing encouragement to collaborate with colleagues and supplying the time and structures to facilitate these opportunities. It also helps if those providing leadership acknowledge and reward teachers for classroom experimentation and reflection.

Within an environment that was conducive to her actions, Maria began her ESL assignment with no overt offers of help. But she found peer assistance and the help of a consultant by tapping her own professional network and making a strong case to her principal that it was in everyone's interests to provide her with more help during the critical first term with her new class. In contrast, Sylvia tried to survive on her own, not even imagining that more help was possible. Isolation exacerbates low teacher self-efficacy, while collaboration is associated with increased confidence and belief in one's self (Tschannen-Moran & Woolfolk Hoy, 2001).

Self-efficacy beliefs also evolve in response to motivational and affective processes. These beliefs influence motivation in several ways. They affect the goals that people set for themselves in the first place: how explicit they are, the effort that is devoted to their achievement, and how long they persevere in the face of obstacles and their resilience to failure. Most theories of motivation award substantial influence to personal goals (see Locke & Latham, 1984).

Motivation also relies on discrepancy reduction and discrepancy production. That is, people are motivated both to reduce the gap between perceived and desired performance and to set themselves challenging enough goals to provide satisfaction and improved self-efficacy when they work hard to accomplish them. For a sense of accomplishment, one's reach ideally exceeds one's grasp initially. Then successfully working through the challenges reinforces one's sense of efficacy. Like Maria, teachers mobilize their skills and effort to accomplish what they seek (Bandura, 1993).

Teachers' beliefs in their own capacities are closely connected to other emotions of interest to us. These beliefs, for example, affect how much stress and depression they experience in threatening or difficult situations and how well they are likely to manage these internal tensions. By the end of the first term, Sylvia—with no support systems in place and alone with her feelings of failure—is close to being burned out, while Maria is tired but has a great sense of accomplishment.

Why Does It Matter?

Our examples of Maria and Sylvia illustrate some of the main reasons why teacher self-efficacy matters. In sum, teachers' beliefs in their ability to perform either a specific task or a more general range of tasks have a strong influence on the amount of effort they expend, how long they persist in trying to accomplish tasks, how resilient they are in the face of failure, and how well they are likely to cope with stress under demanding circumstances (Bandura, 1996). This explanation of how even inaccurate beliefs can produce real capacities has received considerable support from empirical research with teachers. Furthermore, highly self-efficacious teachers also tend to imbue their students with inspiration to reach beyond their grasp. (For a detailed discussion of these ideas, see Schunk & Pajares, 2004.)

Much evidence associates higher levels of teacher self-efficacy with many dimensions of teacher performance in the classroom.[5] Examples include the following:

- Decreased tendencies to be critical of students' incorrect responses and to persist in helping struggling students arrive at correct answers
- Promotion of expectations for achievement in the classroom
- Development of warm interpersonal relationships in the classroom
- An increased tendency to persist with a student failing to understand a concept
- Greater likelihood of grouping students for instruction
- Increased chances of experimenting with instruction
- Greater willingness to try a variety of materials and approaches
- Greater likelihood of implementing innovative practices
- Better planning and organization for instruction
- Increasing chances of treating students fairly
- Increased tendencies to recommend placing lower SES students in a regular classroom
- Openness to educational consultation
- Positive attitudes toward educational reform
- Increased willingness to engage with parents in school
- Higher levels of job satisfaction

---

5. These behaviors are summarized in Goddard & Goddard (2001).

Low levels of teacher self-efficacy, on the other hand, have been associated with an increased probability of leaving the profession (Glickman & Tamashiro, 1982).

A gradually accumulating body of evidence associates higher levels of individual teacher self-efficacy with higher levels of student achievement, particularly in math and reading in the elementary grades and across diverse student populations (Anderson, Greene, & Loewen, 1988; Armor et al., 1976; Ashton & Webb, 1986; Gibson & Dembo, 1984; Ross, 1992). Higher levels of teacher self-efficacy are also associated with more positive student attitudes toward school, subject matter, and teachers. The students of teachers with higher levels of self-efficacy typically have lower rates of suspension and dropping out as well (Esselman & Moore, 1992).

Higher levels of teacher self-efficacy also are associated with higher levels of student self-efficacy, an important mediator of student learning. For example, in a two-year study, Ross et al. (2001) examined the effects of a specific form of teacher efficacy (computer confidence) on students' computer skills and students' self-efficacy. Evidence for the study came from 387 students aged six through nine in 97 classrooms in 46 schools. Ross and his colleagues found that students who moved from a teacher with low computer confidence to a teacher with high computer confidence benefited significantly more from an infusion of technology than students moving from a teacher with high confidence to a teacher with low confidence. The benefits were improved student self-efficacy as well as greater acquisition of computer skills.

What Can Leaders Do About It?

Tschannen-Moran & Barr's (2004) summary of empirical evidence identified seven school conditions, most of which can be shaped by leaders' actions, contributing to individual teacher efficacy:

- Positive school atmosphere
- Academic press among staff
- Sense of community
- Teacher participation in decisions affecting their work
- Lack of barriers to effective instruction
- High expectations for students
- Collaboration among teachers

One of Ross's studies (Ross, McKeiver, & Hogaboam-Gray, 1997) exemplified the results of research about the influence of teacher collaboration, among other things. This was a qualitative study with four exemplary ninth-grade teachers in which teacher efficacy was viewed as a dynamic variable. Results of this study indicated that the introduction of a "destreaming policy" (placing students achieving at different levels in the same classes) initially had negative effects on teacher's sense of efficacy. However, as students began to demonstrate learning comparable to, or better than, their learning in streamed classrooms, teacher efficacy recovered. The working condition accounting most for this recovery was teachers' collaboration with their peers and a timetable that permitted such collaboration. Through collaborative peer relationships, teachers learned new strategies for teaching mixed-ability students, received emotional support, and reduced their workload by not having to reinvent solutions already developed by their colleagues.

In addition to their influence on the school conditions mentioned above, principals emerge in most studies as having a strong, direct influence on teachers' self-efficacy beliefs (Tschannen-Moran et al., 1998; Beatty, 2002). Principals' practices associated with such influence include, for example, being effective intermediators with district superordinates, providing resources for teachers, buffering teachers from disruptions, allowing teachers discretion over classroom decisions, and minimizing student disorder. Principals also positively influence teacher efficacy by helping to develop a shared and inspiring sense of direction for the school, modeling appropriate behavior, and rewarding teachers for success with their students. Most of these practices are subsumed within models of transformational leadership (e.g., Leithwood & Jantzi, 2005). A small handful of studies have tested the effects of this approach to leadership on individual teacher efficacy with promising results (e.g., Hipp, 1996; Hipp & Bredeson, 1995; Mascall, 2003).

Some district conditions have been associated with teacher efficacy. For example, Ross et al.'s (2001) study of computer implementation in the classroom detected a significant influence on teacher efficacy (computer confidence) by well-designed district inservice experiences. In this case, "well-designed" meant that the experience was customized for individual teachers and distributed throughout the period over which computers were being introduced in the curriculum. The improved teacher efficacy led to the establishment of in-school learning support networks and fostered a focus on instructional rather than hardware issues.

COLLECTIVE TEACHER EFFICACY (CTE)

There is an emerging body of research about collective teacher efficacy, reflecting recent interest in the concept. Although the evidence base is small, it is nevertheless generally of good quality and provides robust results. Evidence for this section is based on seven original empirical studies, published between 1998 and 2005, along with two recent reviews of research focused on teachers and schools (Goddard, Hoy, & Woolfolk Hoy, 2000; Tschannen-Moran et al., 1998).

What Is It?

Group or collective efficacy is analogous to, and grows out of, the same theoretical grounding as individual teacher efficacy, a grounding substantially developed by Bandura (1997). Collective efficacy in schools "refers to the perceptions of teachers in a school that the faculty as a whole can execute the courses of action necessary to have positive effects on students" (Goddard, 2001, p. 467). A sense of shared purpose and collective connectedness, precursors to collective efficacy, are exemplified in this comment from a third-grade teacher we interviewed:

> If I had a new teacher come into [our school], I would say, "Don't worry, everything is going to work out." . . . I feel like this school is a family . . . like it's a community.

Another set of comments from a third-grade teacher in a different school and state provides a more extensive expression of collective efficacy:

> We most definitely have one of the best schools in the state, possibly even one of the best in the country. I mean, I think our students have brought that to our community and have brought that to our school. Our students bring that to our school. But our teachers, too. I hear some teachers talking about their kids in other school situations that aren't nearly as nice as ours, or there is difficulty with the teacher being very demanding, doesn't have the time to care, and that makes me realize, "Wow I take this for granted." I just assume that we are all this caring, we are all this flexible, we are all here for the kids. Some places, that is not the case. I take that for granted because we have that. [Staff] converse with one another on a personal level, on a professional level. I mean, there is very little conflict. There is a lot of sharing of ideas. I work with a first-grade teacher also, and we bring our students together once a week to direct activities and reading with the first graders, and so there is collaboration between grade levels so you can go in feeling very comfortable.

A closely related concept, "team potency," has been examined in a small body of research carried out in nonschool contexts (e.g., Boies & Howell, 2006) with results that mirror evidence about collective self-efficacy.

The positive effects of collective efficacy beliefs on the performance of a group of teachers are explained by how those beliefs shape teachers' behaviors and norms. People working in organizations, even those who may do their jobs in relative isolation, are part of a culture and climate that has its own ethos. The relative optimism of an organization's ethos can have a profound impact on the inner experience of its individual members (Beatty, 2002). So when most teachers in the school believe that, together, they can be successful in teaching their students, there is a high level of social expectation that they will do what is necessary to achieve success. In this way, a collective sense of efficacy influences all teachers to persist in their attempts to succeed. While initial efforts may be unsuccessful, persistence in learning is regularly associated with connecting and collaborating with others. These connections create better opportunities for ongoing problem solving and the refinement of teaching practices, which in turn reinforce the shared sense of collective self-efficacy until all are successful.

Adapted from earlier work on individual teacher efficacy (Tschannen-Moran et al., 1998), the most fully developed model of collective teacher efficacy assumes that it is both task- and situation-specific. This means that teachers' sense of collective efficacy depends not only on the nature of the task to be accomplished (e.g., implementing the government's new primary literacy curriculum) but also on key features of the context in which teachers work (e.g., the proportion of ESL students in the school or the extent and quality of relevant professional development they expect to receive from the district). It also depends on the extent to which individual effectiveness is noticed, acknowledged, celebrated, and culturally connected to the shared sense of collective teacher efficacy.

Why Does It Matter?

Differences among schools in the strength of collective teacher efficacy have been associated with variations in both students' mathematics and reading achievement in three studies (Goddard, 2001; Goddard et al., 2000; Tschannen-Moran & Barr, 2004). The most recent of these studies was carried out in 66 Virginia urban, suburban, and rural middle schools. Tschannen-Moran and Barr found significant effects of teachers' collective efficacy on eighth-grade students' writing achievement after controlling for students' socioeconomic status; no effects on math and English achievement were detected, however. Another study reminds us of the situation mentioned earlier in this chapter, in which daunting SES and family conditions external to the school were lowering the collective and individual sense of self-efficacy of the teaching staff (Goddard, 2001). And in yet another study, we see the power of collective efficacy to overcome even the persistent negative impact of low SES on student attainment (Goddard et al., 2000). Importantly, the quality of professional learning and the focus on teaching contribute to the high level of collective teacher efficacy (CTE).

One school with an atypical pattern of high CTE and high attainment despite low SES was studied in depth (Parker, Hannah, & Topping, 2006). In this school climate, or ethos, high-quality in-service training and a focus upon pedagogy were perceived as the most potent factors in raising attainment. When these factors serve to heighten CTE, the impact of SES on pupil attainment may be reduced, although this may be easier in some subjects than others.

What Can Leaders Do About It?

As in the case of individual teacher efficacy, collective efficacy is believed to arise from four sources (Bandura, 1997). The
first and most important of these sources is teachers' prior experiences of success or mastery. A school's past successes and failures
is likely to have a significant effect on teachers' feelings of collective efficacy in approaching new challenges. In his study of 452
teachers from 47 urban elementary schools, Goddard (2001) found
significant effects of mastery experiences on teacher collective
efficacy. Indeed, feelings of mastery arising from past successful
experiences explained about two-thirds of the variation across
schools in collective teacher efficacy. Furthermore, collective mastery experiences far outweighed the effects of students' prior
achievement and such student characteristics as socioeconomic
status, race, and ethnicity.

Bandura (1997) has argued that mastery experiences for groups
of teachers are a function of a number of working conditions, including the following:

- Significant participation in school decision making
- Feedback on the group's performance, perhaps by school or
  district leaders
- Clear and explicit goals for judging the group's success
- "Strong" leadership, which creates a sense of common pur-
  pose or vision for the school

A second source of collective teacher efficacy is vicarious experiences. Such experiences may include, for example, the observation
of other groups of teachers successfully engaged in addressing
issues considered salient to one's school. Social persuasion is a third
source of teacher efficacy. Colleagues or those in leadership roles
may persuade a group of teachers that they have the capacities to
address new challenges successfully (Beatty, 2000b).

Leaders can create support structures and reward systems that
promote the use of study groups among teachers in their schools.
They can also make sure that they communicate the learnings from
these groups to the whole faculty by having groups share their work
and inviting others to develop their own study groups. In so doing,
such leaders effect a shift in culture toward learning together and
integrating the personal professional and organizational self, which

not only increases teachers' self-efficacy (Beatty, 2000b) but also goes a long way toward reducing the intrapersonal and interpersonal tensions that can lead to burnout.

Finally, teachers' other shared feelings have an influence on efficacy. High levels of stress, perhaps even burnout for some group members, will seriously diminish the group's sense of collective efficacy. As we noted in Chapter 3, such stress leads to feelings of being "worn out" and substantially reduces energy for taking on new challenges.

School conditions that have been significantly associated with teachers' collective efficacy are reflected especially well in a recent study by Ross, Hogaboam-Gray, & Gray (2004). This study was carried out with 2,170 elementary teachers in 141 schools. In addition to the significant effects of students' prior achievement, Ross and his colleagues found significant effects on teachers' collective efficacy of "school processes that promoted teacher ownership of school directions" (p. 163), including the following:

- Shared school goals
- Shared, schoolwide decision making
- The fit of school improvement plans with teachers' perceptions of school needs
- Empowering leadership

Ross and his colleagues argued that such conditions influence teachers' thoughts about their own mastery experiences, provide teachers with vicarious experiences, are a source of persuasion that they are up to the challenges facing them, and protect teachers from excessively negative emotional states.

Tschannen-Moran and Barr's (2004) summary of evidence suggested that collective teacher efficacy is fostered by principals who

- Are perceived to be instructional leaders
- Seek creative ways to improve instruction
- Listen to teachers
- Promote innovative teaching
- Engage teachers in school improvement decisions
- Create a positive and supportive school climate
- Provide strong/empowering principal leadership
- Are perceived to be influential with superiors

These and other practices are subsumed within the comprehensive transformational model of leadership we referred to earlier (Leithwood & Jantzi, 2005), a model used in the most recent study reported by Ross and Gray (in press). This study collected evidence from 3,074 Ontario teachers in 218 elementary schools to inquire about the relationships among principals' transformational leadership practices (the empowering form of leadership mentioned in their earlier study (Ross & Gray, 2006), teachers' commitment to community partnerships, and teachers' commitment to their schools. Transformational leadership practices had a significant impact on teachers' collective efficacy and both direct and indirect effects on teacher commitment to school and to community partnerships. These practices are the focus of Chapters 7 and 8.

CONCLUSION

We see moving from being a hands-off leader, who leaves the instructional to the teachers, to one who engages with teachers in a rich, collaborative discourse about teaching as essential to having an impact on teacher individual and collective self-efficacy. The message is: Get involved!

Leaders who continuously demonstrate knowledge of the instructional issues facing their teachers and "wade in" with their teachers to address these issues—leaders who provide structure, incentive, and affirmation for teachers who make the most of opportunities for individual and collaborative self-study—set a positive tone. These leaders exude awareness and appreciation of the complexity of successful teaching at the same time as they model curiosity and inquiry about the craft. Their interest in, concern, and caring for teachers' own faith in themselves and optimism about improvement speaks volumes about what really matters in their schools. Some call this "empowering teachers" (Blase & Blase, 2001). What we see is the value of *encouraging teachers to see themselves as having agency,* potency, and the ability to direct their own professional learning.

Teachers who know that they are allowed to be imperfect works-in-progress can afford to engage in bold self-critique, especially if they are fully aware that the principal sees herself this way, too. The role of the leader in setting the scene for continuous improvement is a powerful one that depends on strengthening beliefs, such as self-efficacy, among teachers. In the final analysis, teacher self-efficacy can make all the difference between choosing hope or despair and in deciding whether to engage or not to engage in the challenges of optimizing the learning conditions for all children.

CHAPTER FIVE

To Stay or Go?

Organizational Commitment and Engagement

L eaders need teachers. It's as simple as that. Without teachers' initiative—their willing and generous commitment of time, energy, effort, ideas, and openness to new learning—a school leader today is in real trouble. How does one renew and reinvent education for a changing world without teachers who are "into it"? This chapter explores two sides of what it means for teachers to be into it. First we examine the causes and consequences of teachers' commitment both to their students and to their schools. Then we interrogate the evidence about why teachers leave their schools or the profession altogether and what forms of leadership might encourage them to remain and renew their commitments.

ORGANIZATIONAL COMMITMENT

Our examination of teacher commitment and its significance is based, in the main, upon 3 reviews of research and 16 original empirical studies, 8 of which were undertaken exclusively in schools between 1989 and 2005. One of these reviews was exclusively focused on teachers (Dannetta, 2002) while two were primarily focused on other employee groups (Mathieu & Zajac, 1990; Wright & Bonett, 2002). Together, this evidence suggests that the causes and consequences of commitment to your organization are quite similar no matter where you work.

What Is It?

Commitment, as a general concept, has been defined as "a psychological state identifying the objects the person identifies with or desires to be involved with" (Leithwood, Menzies, & Jantzi, 1994, p. 41). Research on teacher commitment has distinguished three such "objects"—the student, the profession, and the organization—each of which has generated its own more specific definitions.

Teachers' commitment to students and their learning has been defined as "a sense of efficacy, the expectation that students will learn and the willingness to put forth the effort required for student learning to occur" (Kushman, 1992, p. 9). Teachers' commitment to the profession has been defined as "a positive, affective attachment to one's work" (Dannetta, 2002, p. 145).

Teachers' organizational commitment, after Mowday, Steers, and Porter (1979), has been defined as a three-dimensional construct including a strong belief in, and willingness to accept, the organization's goals and values; a definite desire to maintain organizational membership; loyalty; and a willingness to exert considerable effort on behalf of the organization. A very close facsimile of the last of these conceptions of organizational commitment has been explored in an independent line of research under the title of organizational citizenship behavior (OCB).

First proposed by Organ (1990), OCB is about the behavior one would expect of a teacher who has a strong personal commitment to their school. Volunteering for school committees would be one example of such commitment, as would helping other staff when they experience difficulty, monitoring the behavior of students in the hall and the school yard beyond one's own classroom, agreeing to edit the school yearbook, and tutoring students outside of school hours. High levels of OCB are also reflected in altruistic attitudes, courtesy, efforts to resolve conflicts among one's colleagues, representing the school in district and community contexts, and working hard to improve one's own performance for the sake of the school. Strictly speaking, these tasks lie outside of the teacher's contractual obligations. They may even extend beyond the informal but widely agreed-on expectations that are entrenched in the cultural norms of the school (Podsakoff, MacKenzie, Moorman, & Fetter, 2000; Yukl, 1994).

While efforts have been made to tease out the separate sources of influence on commitment to teaching and to the organization, we consider them together in this chapter. The majority of empirical research has been concerned with teachers' organizational commitment and the quite similar concept of organizational citizenship behavior.

Organizational commitment and job satisfaction are closely related states as well. Some evidence suggests that job satisfaction causes organizational commitment and that working conditions have indirect effects on commitment through their influence on job satisfaction (Williams & Hazer, 1986). But there is also contrary evidence. Organizational commitment, this evidence seems to suggest, may develop first as a sort of precondition of job satisfaction (e.g., Bateman & Strasser, 1984). Compared to organizational commitment, job satisfaction is believed to be less stable and to vary more directly and quickly with changing work conditions.

Why Does It Matter?

Teacher commitment has been identified as an influence on student achievement in a relatively small number of studies (e.g., Dannetta, 2002; Kushman, 1992; Rosenholtz, 1989). A more substantial body of research, however, has linked greater organizational commitment to employee retention (Angle & Perry, 1981; Currivan, 2000; Porter, Steers, Mowday, & Boulian, 1974; Williams & Hazer, 1986), job search activities, absenteeism (e.g., Bateman & Strasser, 1984), and perceptions of organizational effectiveness (Hoy & Ferguson, 1985).

Research on organizational citizenship behavior suggests that it has significant effects on the coordination of work, the stability of the organization's performance, and the ability of an organization to adapt well to its external environment—employee productivity, in short (Podsakoff et al., 2000). But experience in schools also demonstrates how the positive feelings underlying OCB can be squandered. Consider what was entailed for teachers who were confronted with the need to make significant changes to their relationships with parents when "school restructuring" was the watchword for education policy makers around the world. The need to establish school councils and to figure out how to get them up and running well (or at least not get in the way) was work that fell almost entirely outside the formal work contract of most teachers. Indeed, school restructuring that essentially downloaded more and new kinds of work to teachers was a largely failed policy initiative precisely because it escalated the amount of work required of teachers unrelated to their teaching. This was work that tested the OCB limits of even the most civic-minded teachers, not to mention that it distracted teachers from their primary job and primary source of fulfillment: fostering student learning. OCBs in the form of discretionary contributions on the part of teachers were essential for schools to adapt to the restructuring agenda. But the agenda itself was arguably based on unreasonable expectations. Even so, the current and appropriate challenge for leaders remains: to engage teachers in contributing to an educational change agenda calling for a wholesale redefinition of the expectations of teachers and teaching itself.

A good example of research providing such evidence is Wright and Bonett's 2002 meta-analysis of 27 studies including a total sample of 3,630 teacher and nonteacher participants. Notably however, despite the fact that organizational commitment was significantly related to job performance, this relationship declined exponentially with employees' tenure. The analysis found that, controlling for employees' average age, the correlations between tenure and organizational commitment were .437, .161, and .041 for 1, 5, and 10 years of tenure, respectively. This finding is in opposition to career development theory, which assumes that increased tenure is associated with increased commitment because of the accrual of increased benefits (pension benefits, for example). But these results are consistent with a view of teaching as a career that is relatively "flat." That is, financial rewards maximize early, the nature of the job often remains static for many (although the students keep changing), and there is often little recognition or reward for greater expertise and experience. But let's face it, nobody goes into teaching to get rich! Teachers are known to be motivated largely by the intrinsic rewards of making a difference in children's lives, as we have noted before and will note again in the next chapter. Declining commitment among seasoned teachers is a serious issue for today's school leaders.

What Can Leaders Do About It?

From an organizational commitment perspective, leaders who recognize the differing needs of teachers, according to the ages and stages of their careers (Huberman, 1988, 1993) among a myriad of other individual factors, are more likely to garner loyalty and solid commitment to whatever the school and its children may need. For instance, when teaching involves not only working with students but also the stimulation of new learning in meaningful collaborations with colleagues, a whole new lease on life can result (Glickman, Gordon, & Ross-Gordon, 2001). While the teacher demographic is shifting, the majority of today's teachers have literally spent their working lives in the job. Acknowledging the importance of contributions by longtime teachers symbolizes the value of their years of commitment to the organization and sends an important message to those coming along behind. And when experienced teachers share the wealth of their wisdom, they enter a whole new field of professional development, which involves the complexities of adult learning (Glickman et al.). In any case, organizational knowledge exchange among members at all stages of their careers invokes a living legacy and acts as a catalyst to succession planning. The provision of encouragement and time for such exchanges also fosters the sense of mutuality that is inherent in real commitment—the teachers to the school, and the school and its leaders to the teachers.

A substantial body of research about the causes of commitment, most of it conducted in nonschool settings, has been guided by "expectancy" and "social exchange" theories. Expectancy theory assumes that employees enter the organization with expectations and values about the organization and the nature of their workplace; new teachers, for example, expect to receive the support they need to teach the best way they know how. Expectations, then, are beliefs about what conditions will characterize the workplace. Values are employees' conceptions of desired outcomes in the workplace. New teachers value making a significant difference in the lives of their students, for example. To the extent that the expectations and values of employees are met, positive emotions (satisfaction) toward their work and commitment to the organization develop (Mathieu & Zajac, 1990).

According to social exchange theory, satisfaction and commitment develop through an exchange of the employer's rewards for employees' work, a kind of quid pro quo relationship. So work orientations are influenced by the degree to which the employer (school, district, principal) is perceived to provide desired rewards. The rewards that teachers most want, however, are the organizational conditions they need to do their best work with their students (Nias, 1989; Nias, Southworth, & Yeomans, 1989)!

A helpful point of departure for understanding the results of this largely nonschool research that is guided by such theories is the meta-analysis of much of it carried out up to 1990 by Mathieu and Zajac (1990). This analysis began with some 48 determinants, correlates, and consequences of commitment, based on 124 published studies, classified as role states, job characteristics, group/leader relations, and organizational characteristics.

With respect to role states, results indicated that commitment was moderately and negatively associated with routinization (lack of variety in the nature of the tasks undertaken), role ambiguity (lack of clarity about one's responsibilities and accountabilities), role conflict (difference of opinion about what the job entails), and excessive workload. Demonstrating a moderately positive relationship with commitment was autonomy in deciding how to carry out one's job along with peer and supervisor support. Higher pay was not a determinant of either satisfaction or commitment.

The job characteristics reviewed in the Mathieu and Zajac meta-analysis (1990) were drawn primarily from Hackman and Oldham's (1975) job characteristics model, which suggests that "enriched" jobs are likely to produce higher levels of organizational commitment. Research previous to that of Mathieu and Zajac typically supported the value of this model. Features of an enriched job, according to this model, are skill variety (results of the meta-analysis indicated a medium positive correlation with commitment), task autonomy (a small positive correlation), challenge (not tested due to lack of data), and job scope (a strong positive correlation).

Results of the meta-analysis also indicated significant, positive relations between organizational commitment and a small handful of group/leader relationships, including the following:

- *Task interdependence.* "When employees experience high functional dependence, they become more aware of their own contributions to the organization and to their immediate work group. This heightened awareness may enhance employees' ego involvement and thereby increase their [organizational commitment]" (Mathieu & Zajac, 1990, pp. 179–180).
- Leader's initiating structure (being clear about what needs to be done and how) and showing consideration for the goals, aspirations, and circumstances of colleagues.

- *Leader communication.* A "supervisor who provides more accurate and timely types of communication enhances the work environment and thereby is likely to increase employees commitment to the organization" (Mathieu & Zajac, p. 180).
- *Participatory leadership.* This means involving teachers in class and school decision making.

Results of the meta-analysis suggested no significant relationships between organizational commitment and the two organizational conditions for which data were available—organizational size and the degree to which decisions are centralized.

Research about organizational commitment conducted with teachers reflects many of the results summarized in Mathieu and Zajac's meta-analysis (1990) but extends these results in ways that reflect the distinctive qualities of teaching and schools. Evidence about the causes of teachers' commitment to student learning can be found in many original sources, such as Kushman (1992), Menzies (1995), Reyes and Imber (1992), and Rosenholtz (1989). In addition to providing original evidence of his own from teachers, Dannetta (2002) also provided a comprehensive review of empirical evidence about factors influencing teachers' commitment to student learning. There is considerable overlap with the results of his review and those of his own study employing both interview and survey methods. Dannetta's review provides the core of the evidence reported here, supplemented with a sample of other relevant original studies.

With respect to role states, Dannetta's (2002) review consistently supported the negative effects of excessive workload on teachers' commitment. It also indicates that the perceived fairness of the workload, not just the amount of work, has an important bearing on teachers' commitment. Teachers, like other employee groups, are more committed to their organizations when they have the autonomy and discretion to shape their work the best way they know how and when they experience little role conflict—when they believe in and accept the value of pursuing their school's goals.

In relation to teachers' job characteristics, Dannetta's (2002) review found substantial indications that organizational commitment was strongly influenced by teachers' perceptions of the meaningfulness of their work along with opportunities for ongoing learning and professional growth. Others have reported the effects on teachers' organizational commitment of perceptions that the job is doable but challenging, the amount of feedback provided to teachers about their performance, and the amount of social interaction and role conflict which they perceive (Buchanan, 1974; Hall, Schneider, & Nygren, 1970).

With reference to group/leader relations, Dannetta (2002) found commitment to be positively influenced by the quality of administrators' leadership, including their flexible enforcement of rules, their buffering of teachers from external distractions, the support they provided to faculty, and their ability to influence district leaders. Commitment also increased with smaller work groups, development of a sense of community with colleagues and administrators, and opportunities to participate in decisions.

Other recent evidence echoes Dannetta's results about group/leader relations. For example, Tsui and Cheng's (2002) study of 423 Hong Kong teachers found that organizational commitment was significantly influenced by principals' "consideration" behaviors. Teachers' commitment was more positive when principals were friendly, open to teachers' suggestions, supportive, and collegial and when the principal looked out for the welfare of faculty members. Teachers with relatively short tenure were more influenced by this condition than were teachers with longer tenure. To these leadership characteristics fostering teacher commitment, Nguni, Sleegers, and Denessen's (2006) study added the provision of a shared vision, a key dimension of transformational approaches to leadership. Nir (2002) also provided evidence of the significant relationship between teachers' organizational commitment and supportive principal behavior. In addition, trust-building leadership behaviors were found to have a significant influence on teachers' OCBs in a recent study using a large sample of U.S. teachers (Banki, 2006).

On the matter of organizational conditions, Dannetta (2002) found that teachers' organizational commitment was reduced by the extra demands on time and energy by government initiatives, such as the implementation of new curricula. It was also reduced by excessive tension in the school created by struggles over competing priorities.

Positive organizational conditions included an orderly school climate and the school's efficient and effective management of student behavior. Additionally, Tsui and Cheng (2002) found that teacher commitment was higher in schools with "institutional integrity." These were schools with well-developed programs suiting the student population that also had the ability to cope successfully with destructive outside forces. The commitment of married teachers, in particular, was influenced by this condition, perhaps because of their family commitments and feelings of greater vulnerability to unreasonable demands from parents and other community members.

Leaders today are called upon to help teachers reenvision the provision of their discretionary time and effort so that they and their colleagues can learn to learn together. Bold self-critique, evidence-based improvement of practice, action research, and involvement in mentoring and peer-coaching programs are typically being adopted as "core" to the business of teaching. The challenge for leaders is clear: integrate OCBs into teachers' redefinition of "professional" and "organizational" citizenship by making membership dependent upon it. While this may sound draconian, no top-down, autocratic version of leadership will accomplish such a transformation. To enter this territory with any chance of surviving and, better still, thriving, leaders need to reenvision leadership itself, as learning for everyone, including themselves! In this way, schools can literally become learning organizations, places where what needs to be known and understood emerges through genuine cooperative inquiry. Norms of respectful communication, openness to critical friendship, and reciprocal learning at all levels are endemic in such schools. All members are moved by new ideas and new learning and the social and emotional rewards of membership in an efficacious group.

To establish the norms we have identified, it is important to model open learning reciprocity. To accomplish this, "one must be open to influence, to being emotionally 'moved,' to being vulnerable" (Jordan, 1993, p. 1). Leaders need to overcome illusions of self-sufficiency and the excessive need for power and control. To accomplish this, they need to learn how to manage proactively their own inevitably confronting emotional experiences of vulnerability and uncertainty. Leaders who ignore or deny these often frightening emotional realities can put themselves and everyone else at risk.

> Denial of vulnerability and the movement into a power/control mode can lead to a relational pattern of entitlement, self-preoccupation, and failure of empathy in one persona and accommodation, compliance, and silencing in the other. While giving the appearance of connection, inauthenticity and a deep sense of disconnection prevail (Miller, 1998; Miller & Stiver, 1991; Stiver, 1990). At its extreme, we see this pattern in many abusive relationships. (Jordan, 1993)

Without the conscious acknowledgment and active pursuit of learning about their own uncomfortable emotions, by default, leaders can inadvertently damage the very processes they wish to foster. We will say more about leader emotions in our final chapter.

ENGAGEMENT AND DISENGAGEMENT IN THE SCHOOL OR PROFESSION

This section is based on evidence from one review of research (Macdonald, 1999) and 15 original empirical studies conducted between 1986 and 2005.

What Is It?

The concept of engagement or disengagement is used here as a means of bringing together the results of a line of research about the incidence of teachers' changing schools or leaving the profession. This evidence is about the causes of attrition from schools or the profession rooted in several of the internal states reviewed in this and earlier chapters, in particular, job satisfaction and organizational commitment.

Why Does It Matter?

Recent reports of teacher attrition generally agree that it is fairly high. For example, Buckley, Schneider, and Shang (2005) reported that one quarter of all U.S. teachers leave the profession within four years, and a recent Ontario study (Matsui & Lang Research, 2005) found that one in three elementary teachers were actively considering leaving the profession. But the consequences of this attrition are far from obvious, except in the threshold case of being unable to find sufficient numbers of replacements. Taking a broad international perspective on the issue, Macdonald (1999) cited a number of clearly negative effects, including discontinuity of staff within schools engaged in systematic improvement initiatives, reduction in quality of teaching staff when the most qualified leave in disproportionately large numbers, and an aging profile of teachers when a significant proportion of new teachers leave. But as Macdonald pointed out, positive outcomes are also possible. Positive outcomes might include the redistribution of skilled workers to other segments of the job market and the return to the profession of teachers who temporarily leave, bringing with them useful new skills and experiences. A positive outcome would also be the elimination of resistance to change when those who leave do so because they object to policy changes or school improvement directions. While each of these possible positive and negative outcomes of attrition has been observed, there is no reliable data about the incidence of each.

What Can Leaders Do About It?

Considerable evidence suggests that decisions by teachers to leave their schools or the profession are influenced especially by job satisfaction and organizational commitment (e.g., Stockard & Lehman, 2004). So most of the working conditions associated with these internal states also contribute to teacher retention or attrition. Nonetheless, a significant amount of research focuses directly on teacher attrition and retention. This section of the chapter examines the working conditions emerging from a sample of such research. In the United States, many of these studies have depended on data collected by the National Center for Educational Statistics, part of the U.S. Department of Education, through its periodically administered *School and Staffing Surveys* and *Teacher Follow-Up Surveys*.

Excellent examples of studies making productive use of these data are those reported by Ingersoll (2001a, 2001b). His studies were based on evidence from a large sample (6,733) of U.S. teachers responding to recent administrations of both of the National Center's surveys. At the time of the study, this was "the largest and most comprehensive data source available on the staffing, occupational, and organizational aspects of schools" (2001b, p. 9) and was considered nationally representative. Results of this study indicated that teacher turnover was predicted by three categories of variables:

- *Teacher characteristics.* Turnover was more likely among both older (over 50) and younger (under 30) teachers, as well as minority and female teachers.
- *School size and sector.* Teachers were more likely to leave smaller rather than larger, private rather than public schools, urban rather than suburban or rural schools, and elementary rather than secondary schools. Within public schools alone,

"teachers in suburban schools are slightly more likely to turnover than those in urban public schools, once other factors are controlled. School size and district size are both inversely related to turnover in public schools" (Ingersoll, 2001b, p. 19).

- *Organizational conditions.* After controlling for the characteristics of teachers and schools, teacher retention was associated with higher salaries, support from administrators, a positive disciplinary climate, and opportunities for teachers to participate in school decision making.

The organizational conditions identified by Ingersoll of most interest to us in this book have been confirmed and extended in a substantial number of other studies of teacher retention and attrition. For example, in their study of turnover among California teachers, Loeb, Darling-Hammond, and Luczak found that high levels of staff turnover are a function of low salaries, large class sizes, problems with facilities, multitrack schools, and lack of textbooks. When these conditions are taken into account, "the influence of student characteristics on turnover is substantially reduced" (2005, p. 45).

Other studies included in our review identified the following working conditions associated with teachers actually leaving their school or district or quitting the profession:

- Low salaries, especially relative to other nearby districts (e.g., Loeb, 2001; Pogodzinski, 2000; Theobald, 1990)
- Employment opportunities outside teaching (e.g., Ingersoll, 2001a)
- Leadership style of principal and/or lack of support from school administrators (Bempah, Kaylen, Osburn, & Birkenholz, 1994; Wright, 1991)
- Lack of autonomy (Shen, 1997)
- Lack of influence on school decisions (Shen)
- Inadequate facilities (e.g., Seyfarth & Bost, 1986)
- Student characteristics: for example, race, apathy, indiscipline, and low achievement (e.g., Hanushek, Kain, & Rivkin, 2001)
- Lack of access to professional development (Hirsch, 2004a, 2004b)
- Low status of the profession in the community (e.g., Buckley et al., 2005)
- Poor relationships with parents and the community (e.g., Buckley et al.)

- Negative images of teaching in the popular media (Buckley et al.)
- Class load, including average class size and teaching outside one's area of certification (e.g., Mont & Rees, 1996)
- Burden of nonteaching duties (Buckley et al.)
- Government policies (erratic and unresponsive) creating confusion and uncertainty (Buckley et al.)
- Accountability and increased use of high-stakes tests (e.g., Tye & O'Brien, 2002)

A recently reported study undertaken in England with 300 teachers in 100 schools (Day, Stobart, Sammons, Kington, Gu, et al., 2006) investigated factors that influence teacher identity based on the premise that identity has a substantial influence on self efficacy, motivation, commitment, job satisfaction, and effectiveness. This study inquired about the reasons for variation in teacher effectiveness at different stages of their careers across a wide variety of schools. Results of this study indicated the following:

- There is a statistically significant association between the levels of pupil progress and attainment in English and math and the extent to which teachers sustain their commitment.
- The quality of leadership both at school and department level, relationships with colleagues, and personal support are key factors influencing teachers' motivation, self-efficacy, commitment, and quality relations.
- A major challenge to motivation and commitment was the difficulty of managing a heavy workload along with commitments in their personal lives.
- Many teachers found it difficult to maintain their motivation in the face of government policies and initiatives, which were often viewed negatively.
- Finally, teachers most able to sustain their motivation, commitment, and sense of efficacy were often found in primary schools serving more-advantaged students.

CONCLUSION

We know that the long-term professional commitment and engagement of teachers is largely a function of the success they experience in their classrooms and the consequent bolstering of their belief in themselves and the worth of the work that they do. To address performance issues that interfere with success, teachers need assurances that their dignity is safe and that they are valued within their organizations. Maintaining a teacher's spirit of generosity for giving and giving over a professional lifetime is something of a balancing act. Many variables are in play. Recent research is showing, however, that leaders can be the deciding factor, creating the tipping point in a teacher's ability to summon the strength to go back to the drawing board, to persevere for improvement—or not.

As teachers' work and expectations of that work develop throughout their careers in response to a changing world, teachers are bound to be affected by the working conditions that foster or frustrate their intentions. These conditions have everything to do with the decisions that leaders make every day. Whether or not teachers choose to "renew their membership" from year to year can have a great deal to do with the perceptions they have about their leaders' perceptions of them (Beatty, 2002). School leaders who get out of their offices and into respectful, caring conversations, which help teachers see themselves within the bigger picture of new policies and the organization as a whole, make an important difference. So do leaders who stimulate creativity and encourage discovery and professional growth. Leaders build commitment and engagement when they share governance and foster collaborative, learning-focused cultures that are resilient and adept at solving problems (Blase & Blase, 2001).

CHAPTER SIX

From Feeling to Acting

Teacher Motivation and
Educational Reform

I n this chapter, we extend our understanding about the nature and consequences of teacher emotions by examining theories and evidence about teacher motivation. This chapter describes the nature and sources of teacher motivation. It also illustrates the influence of several widely advocated policy and reform initiatives on such motivation. We believe the framework used in this chapter for understanding teacher motivation can be of considerable practical value to school leaders as they think about their own efforts to support their teaching colleagues.

We are inclined to think of conditions in teachers' local environments as having the greatest impact on their feelings. Much has been made, for example, of just how satisfying and efficacy-inducing teachers find day-to-day indications of their students' progress (e.g., Lortie, 1975) and how disconnected at least some teachers feel about schoolwide matters (Beatty, 2002). This impression might have as much to do with the selected focus of researchers who study and write about what teachers' feel strongly about as it does with the full range of teachers' concerns. Nonetheless, there is evidence that teachers and leaders typically do not discuss their individual concerns with each other, a condition that creates and maintains the distance between them (Beatty, 2005). This may have further impacts on their motivations. Alternatively, such discussions could strengthen shared understandings and enhance the possibilities for the motivations of teachers and leaders to become more closely linked (Beatty, 2002).

What Is Motivation?

In commonsense terms, whatever prompts people to act as they do is motivational. It is a soupy mix of thoughts and feelings. So job satisfaction, commitment, engagement, morale, and most of the other emotions described in earlier chapters can be considered part of the conceptual net cast by the concept "motivation." But these feelings alone don't tell the whole story, because what people do is a product not only of their feelings but their thinking as well.

It is almost impossible to separate thoughts from feelings. Most of our ideas include both. Sometimes we give greater weight to one over the other in our decisions to act. Consider how often we find ourselves doing things we don't actually like—hauling ourselves out of bed when the alarm goes off or wading through paperwork and preparing for the week ahead on Sunday afternoon. We do these things not because we feel like doing them but because we think they should be done and feel obligated to do them. On the other hand, we often find ourselves doing things we think we shouldn't because it feels so good at the time—eating too much ice cream, consuming too much alcohol, driving too fast. Our actions are motivated by a soupy mixture of both emotions and thoughts, something of a seamless blend of thinking and feeling (Damasio, 1997).

A synthesis of two formal accounts of motivation (see Pittman, 1998) forms the understanding of motivation we outline in this chapter. One view explains the motivational processes associated with teachers' constructions of their understanding, or mental representations of the world. This approach focuses our attention on the attributions and related judgments teachers make about, for example, the outcomes and intentions of government educational policies (Are these policies sensible? Will they help?).

The second view of motivation aims to explain how motivation affects people's overt actions (see Bandura, 1990; Ford, 1992). Teachers' actions, from this perspective, are shaped by their personal goals ("I really want to make some progress with my kids' understanding of numbers this year"), beliefs about their capacities (the efficacy beliefs we described in Chapter 4), beliefs about one's context ("Do I have access to the resources I need?"), and emotional arousal processes (actions prompted by many of the feelings described in earlier chapters and elsewhere). Both approaches to motivation include a central role for teacher emotions, and both attach considerable importance to teachers' goals and intentions.

Goals

Personally valued goals for one's work are the objects of a person's commitment and engagement, representing desired future states (aspirations, needs, wants, interests) that have been internalized by an individual. Goals energize action toward, for example, the implementation of government accountability policies when a teacher's evaluation of present circumstances indicates that they are different from what she would like them to be. And goals energize action when they are perceived to be hard but achievable ("I want to use heterogeneous groupings in my class, rather than the homogeneous groups I use now, although most of my students are not going to like it to begin with.")

To have motivational effects, goals also must be clear and concrete and include interim goals for the short term that are understood within the context of longer-term and, perhaps more importantly, more obviously valuable goals ("If I can get kids who are achieving at different levels to help one another in my classroom, they are likely to develop the skills they will need to work productively in teams in their future places of work") (see Bandura, 1986; Locke, Latham, & Eraz, 1988).

As we have pointed out many times already, the most often cited goals motivating teachers are typically intrinsic in nature, helping students learn and seeing them being successful (Goodlad, 1984; Lortie, 1975). Nonetheless, intrinsic and extrinsic goals interact. While teachers primarily are motivated by intrinsic goals, money matters, especially to teachers whose pay falls short of personal needs (Ozcan, 1996). Johnson (1998) distinguished three problems that require different orientations to teacher goals: attracting people into the profession, retaining them once there, and engaging them in improving their own performance. Most relevant to this chapter, the third goal requires the orchestration of organizational opportunities that encourage teachers to think about their work in new ways and commit themselves to new standards and goals. We envision a combination of extrinsic and intrinsic incentives. According to Johnson's review of evidence, these incentives should "coordinate teachers' efforts, provide them with shared purpose, enhance the conditions of their work, and reaffirm their professional identity" (p. 74). As Nias (1989) and Beatty (2000b) have noted, teachers need conditions that help them achieve their core purposes if they are to access the intrinsic rewards of their work.

Several recent studies carried out in school reform contexts further clarify the nature of teacher goals in the face of educational reform initiatives. Studying the implementation of the whole school reform Success For All (SFA), Datnow and Castellano (2000) found further evidence of the primacy of intrinsic goals for teachers. SFA appealed to many teachers because they believed it did a good job of helping their students learn to read (the teachers' dominant goal), even though it was hard to implement. Kelley and Protsik (1997) and Heneman (1998) inquired about teacher motivation in response to pay-for-performance policies in Kentucky and Tennessee, respectively. Both studies reported that bonuses, while appreciated by teachers as a form of recognition and a source of pride, had no "before-the-fact" motivational value. The performance-based measures used in Kentucky focused, more than did those in Tennessee, on clarity, reliability, content, fairness, and teaching to the test. As a result, these measures caused more extensive change in classroom instruction than did the tests used for determining bonuses in Tennessee.

Kentucky teachers also were acutely aware of negative sanctions prompted by poor test results (including state intervention in the management of schools and dismissal of teachers) and were anxious to avoid them. Firestone, Mayrowetz, and Fairman's (1998) comparison of the effects on instruction of performance-based assessment in Maine and Maryland produced results very similar to those found in Kentucky and Tennessee.

While teachers seem primarily motivated by the goal of reaching their students, even in the context of specific reforms that are difficult to implement, other, more extrinsic goals also come into play. When reforms are accountability oriented and the stakes are high, teachers' intrinsic goals may be partly displaced by such extrinsic goals as money and "winning" the school's ranking competition. This shift in motivational goals may have nontrivial consequences. Teachers who are constrained in ways likely to reduce their own intrinsic motivation to teach may behave in more controlling ways and be less effective in teaching their students. Furthermore, perceptions of the teacher as intrinsically motivated increase the chances of students being intrinsically motivated as well (Pittman, 1998).

Capacity Beliefs

Such psychological states as self-efficacy, self-confidence, self-concept, and aspects of self-esteem are included in the term *capacity beliefs*. As we discussed in Chapter 4, it is important that people believe themselves to be capable of accomplishing their goals. But they also need to have a compelling desire to achieve them (in addition to the skill, of course). Contributions of self-efficacy to motivation are worth exploring; beliefs about personal teaching efficacy influence students through the type of classroom environment teachers create (Bandura, 1993). Teachers model hope, confidence, perseverance—and the lack of these qualities. Their beliefs in their own ability to "get through" to their students can transfer to children's beliefs in themselves. The motivation that both leads to and flows from self-efficacy is part of a reinforcing spiral of cause and effect. Perceived self-efficacy increases the intrinsic value of effort and contributes to a sense of collective efficacy on the part of the group as well (Goddard, Hoy, & Woolfolk, 2000). In a highly self-efficacious teacher culture, the motivation to strive in the face of tall odds can come from the motivation for membership. To belong, one is expected to strive and to succeed. There is no room for giving up in schools that enjoy collective efficacy. This may help to explain why teachers' sense of collective efficacy has been associated with improved student achievement (Bandura, 1993; Goddard et al., 2000). Teachers' beliefs about their individual professional efficacy are significantly related to the effectiveness of their classroom practices, student learning, and the likelihood that they will engage in classroom and school improvement initiatives (Ross, 1998; Smylie, 1990).

As you will recall from Chapter 4, teachers' beliefs in their capabilities, their efficacy beliefs, are influenced by such variables as school size, sense of control over classroom conditions, sense of community, teaching assignment, the nature of the school's culture, and feedback from colleagues and supervisors (Lee, Dedrick, & Smith, 1991; Ross, 1998). In quite different school reform contexts, both Heneman (1998) and Kelley and Protsik (1997) reported that teachers were influenced by the confidence they had in their ability to implement the necessary changes in their practices. Successful teachers perceived a link between their efforts and subsequent improvements in student achievement. It is one thing to have the capacity to do something, another to believe you are capable of doing something, another to want to do it enough to try, and still another to want to succeed enough to persevere in the face of adversity.

The distinctions among a range of capability beliefs, such as self-efficacy, and their links with motivation have been considered by Pajares (1996). He concluded from his review of evidence that "students need to have both the 'will' and the 'skill' to be successful in classrooms" (Pajares, as cited in Pintrich & De Groot, 1990, p. 38). Teachers do too! Self-efficacy is essential, but it is predictive of action only when positive motivation and follow-through accompany it.

Bandura's (1986) concept of "triadic reciprocity" among behavioral, environmental, and personal factors reminds us of the interdependency of such factors as self-efficacy, self-concept, and motivation and actions or behavior and the environment. Triadic reciprocity speaks to the delicate and dynamic interdependency of teacher working conditions (environment) with self-efficacy, motivation, and sense of agency (personal factors) along with actions toward performance (behavior). Successful behavior feeds self-efficacy through its provision of evidence of "skill," which can in turn strengthen the "will," or motivation to persevere in the work and continue the process of improving further. Ford (1992) suggested that motivation is a combination of energy source and energy direction for future orientation and persistence. Pintrich and Schunk (2002) synthesized these ideas in a simple equation, Motivation = Goals × Emotions × Personal Agency Beliefs. The use of the multiplier symbol suggests that "if any of these three components is missing, individuals will not be motivated in that situation"; that is, "if they do not have a goal activated or have very negative inhibitory affect or have a very low belief in their personal capabilities, motivation will be very low and the behavior will likely be terminated for that situation" (p. 199).

Why Does It Matter?

Evidence (see Jones & Davis, 1965; Pittman, 1998; Weiner, 1990) suggests that the meaningfulness of such things as government accountability policies begins with teachers' judgments about the anticipated or actually experienced desirability of the outcomes that a new policy intends to achieve. When a policy is judged to have desirable consequences, it is likely to be viewed favorably for implementation, provided that teachers perceive such outcomes to be relevant to their work ("It won't take as long for me to complete these new report cards as it did the old ones.") and that they believe policy makers both intended such outcomes and are responsible for their achievement.

Teachers are likely to reject a policy as not meaningful under exactly the same set of conditions, except for a judgment of actual outcomes as undesirable. ("The government's mainstreaming policy was very well intentioned, with lots of promise theoretically, but it just doesn't work in practice.") This judgment may well give rise to feelings of anger and frustration, although these feelings will be less extreme when the government is understood to have been constrained in some way by factors outside its control ("They just didn't have the money to hire the teacher aids needed to make the policy work.").

But when the government is viewed as acting in a largely unconstrained environment (e.g., access to sufficient money), with other motives suspected, extremely negative evaluations are likely to occur. These evaluations will be even more extreme if the government is also viewed as generally undervaluing school professionals and their work.

Teachers' beliefs and judgments about government intentions may be more or less accurate. Evidence suggests that a teacher's ability to make sense of a policy influences that teacher's emotional states positively or negatively (Leithwood, Jantzi, & Steinbach, 2002). These emotional states, in turn, have a bearing on the degree to which the teacher will be concerned about the accuracy of his understandings. Frustration with a policy, for example, may limit the amount of effort a teacher is willing to devote to understand its implications fully. Such accuracy is further influenced by expectations of future interactions with the other person or group (in this case, the government) and the extent to which one is dependent on this interaction for important outcomes ("Why bother wasting my time trying to implement this new policy? The elections are near, and this government is likely to lose."). Also influencing accuracy concerns is personal accountability for justifying one's attitudes or inferences, the importance of the task, and a number of personal qualities, such as desire for control and the need for closure and structure.

The experience of lack of control or understanding has two effects: an increased desire to regain understanding or potential control and an increased desire to avoid the negative implications of any further loss of control. If increased attention, effort, and thought seem likely to succeed, then accuracy motivation will predominate. If not, the teacher may initiate ego-protective measures, such as self-handicapping (e.g., not bothering to read about the policy), or fall prey to illusions and biases ("These people have no idea what will work in my classroom") as part of the price of defensive behavior.[6] The motivation to understand a new policy accurately, furthermore, will be highest during the process of deciding what to do (e.g., to begin implementing or to ignore), whereas motivationally compatible illusions are more likely when one has decided to act and is in the process of acting ("I am not going to worry about developing heterogeneous groups in my class because no one else in my school is doing it.").[7]

Context Beliefs

As we indicated earlier in the chapter, teachers' capacity beliefs are influenced by such features of their context as school size, sense of community, teaching assignment, and feedback from colleagues and leaders. Additional features of the context influence teacher motivation in some educational policy or reform contexts, however. As a result of previous mismanaged, ill-conceived, or short-lived initiatives for change, many experienced teachers have developed considerable skepticism about how supportive the school context will be for their implementation efforts (Huberman, 1988). Consistent with the theories discussed above, negative context beliefs created by these past experiences easily may graft themselves onto teachers' perceptions of current reform initiatives, thereby

---

6. Of course, there are many instances in which teachers quite appropriately reject government policy initiatives in the best interests of their students. This is not the context we have in mind here.

7. Although it seems likely that teachers' perceived policy outcomes are influenced by what school leaders do, we are unaware of research exploring the matter.

eroding the motivation to implement such reforms. Leaders become important agents of interpretation here.

Recent studies of school reform identify specific features of the context affecting the motivation of teachers. Datnow and Castellano (2000) found that some teachers were positively influenced by their belief that the Success for All program created consistency across the school in the way teachers were able to talk to one another about the teaching of reading. Implementation also was aided by the strong support perceived by teachers from the principal, the facilitator, and the SFA trainers. In their study of reform in San Diego, California, McLaughlin and Mitra (2001) found that how the reform was introduced "soured people from believing in the benefits of the 'what,' causing teacher resistance, animosity, and angst within some schools" (p. 3). Furthermore, some teachers resisted the initiative because they believed there was insufficient evidence to support the positive effects claimed by the reformers. Heneman's (1998) investigation of teacher responses to a school-based performance-award program found that teachers were influenced by the availability of resources, curriculum alignment, team teaching and planning opportunities, professional development, and parent support for their work. Leaders who integrate this knowledge of teachers' thoughts and feelings about reforms into their collaborative consideration with teachers help to engender a sense of shared purpose that, with collective efficacy, adds to motivation. Leaders' deliberate and carefully positioned provision of professional development opportunities, when presented in the spirit of respect, care, and professional support, can be powerfully motivating as well (Beatty, 2002). Receiving best practice information was an important feature of the context in studies by both Heneman (1998) and Kelley and Protsik (1997).

Principals' leadership has a more significant effect on teachers' context beliefs than it has on the three other sources of motivation included in our framework (Leithwood, 1994; Earl et al, 2001). Positive context beliefs by teachers are associated with such school leadership practices as helping to clarify the reasons for implementing the policy, empowering teachers to participate in decisions about how the policy will be implemented, providing resources to assist such implementation, and making available opportunities to acquire the new skills necessary for policy implementation (Leithwood & Jantzi, in press).

Emotional Arousal Processes

The motivation for teachers to act in a particular way is influenced by their emotions and feelings, some of which have been described at length in earlier chapters. Some of these emotions are prompted by teachers' judgments about the desirability of the outcomes associated with new policies or other reform initiatives they are asked to implement (as well as capacity and context beliefs). Some of these emotions are prompted by the sense that they are cared for by their leaders (Beatty, 2002). These emotions influence the accuracy of teachers' understandings, as well as serving to maintain or discontinue such patterns of teacher action as policy implementation.

Teachers' engagement from day to day in such actions will be sustained by a positive emotional climate, which is strongly related to leaders' approaches to decision making and communication (Blase & Anderson, 1995). Conditions supporting such a climate are also likely to include, for example, frequent positive feedback from parents and students about their experiences with the school's change initiatives, frequent positive feedback from one's teaching colleagues about one's success in achieving short-term goals associated with change initiatives, and a dynamic and changing job (Ozcan, 1996).

Positive emotions help teachers persist in attempting to accomplish long-range goals, even when evidence of progress is meager. But they can also be subordinated in the service of goals considered more central to teachers' motivation. Datnow and Castellano (2000) found that the structured and highly prescribed nature of Success for All was viewed by some teachers as boring, monotonous, demeaning, and generally interfering with their enjoyment and creativity. Some teachers adapted the program extensively for this reason. But some endured their negative feelings because they felt the program was helpful for kids, and that mattered more to these teachers than their own enjoyment.

Firestone et al. (1998) found weak "avoidance of shame" responses on the part of teachers and administrators faced with high-stakes state testing policies. While the stakes were not exceptionally high in the context for this study, educators clearly wished to avoid the embarrassment that would accompany the failure of the school to score adequately on the tests. So they were inclined to make relatively superficial changes in their practices that would ensure success, rather than the more fundamental changes in their practices that were called for by the reform.

School leaders contribute to the positive valence of teacher emotions by complimenting teachers on good work, requesting their advice on important matters, and ensuring that they publicly make others inside and outside the school aware of teachers' contributions to the success of the school. These are honorific rewards that can produce feelings of enjoyment, satisfaction, and happiness when they are interpreted by teachers as evidence of appreciation and respect for their work (Beatty, 2002, 2007a; Johnson, 1998; Ozcan, 1996).

CONCLUSION

In this chapter, we have featured the impact of motivation of teachers, along with the "flow-on" effects and synergies with self-efficacy, on teachers' desire to succeed. The impact of highly motivated teachers upon their students is clear. Motivation is the source of energy that sustains improvement efforts in our schools. Motivations of leaders and teachers—both in level and direction—can combine for good effect or create tensions and disincentives that undermine success. When the motivations of policy makers and leaders themselves are considered to be suspect, all manner of undesirable side effects can occur. These arise from spurious emotionality (Denzin, 1984) and corresponding misinterpretations of each other, which undermine the solvency of relationships and create an emotional complexity that can be difficult to unravel if leaders and teachers don't talk about it.

The power of "emotional meaning making" (Beatty, 2002, p. 12), the process of discussing explicitly how both leaders and teachers are feeling about the weight of perceived expectations of them, can create social and emotional common ground and a shared understanding of the context they occupy together. In the final chapter, we will examine in more detail the emotional dynamics of the teacher-leader relationship. The complexities of a person's own motivations necessarily involves interpretations about the motives of others. The projection of imagined, unconfirmed, or unconfirmable motivations can complicate the situation considerably. We suggest that leaders reflect more on their own motivations, future orientations, and levels of self-efficacy and agency as well as their own feelings about all of these self-constructs. Such self-reflection is fundamental to the development of authentic leader-teacher relationships.

CHAPTER SEVEN

Leading With Teacher Emotions in Mind

Setting Directions and Developing People

> *The principal influences everything.... It's more than how I relate to teachers ... it affects everything across the board: motivation, morale, feelings, relations with students ... parents ... how you relate to kids.... Effective principals are ones who make a positive climate.... An ineffective person can destroy everything. (Direct quotation from a teacher in Blase & Anderson, 1995, p. 66)*

As accounts of teacher emotions described in earlier chapters suggest, many organizational conditions influence those emotions. Leadership practices, usually those of principals, have emerged repeatedly as among the most consequential of those conditions. However, very little of the research on which earlier chapters are based actually began with a focus on leadership. The vast majority of this research "discovered" or "tripped over" leadership among a wide array of other variables giving rise to teacher emotions. For this reason, the actual leadership practices with positive consequences for how teachers feel about their work have rarely been viewed as part of a formal model or theory of leadership.

Nonetheless, accumulating the leadership practices that have been identified piecemeal across the many studies of teacher emotions produces an unmistakably "transformational" picture of emotionally consequential leadership, an outcome foreshadowed in Chapter 1. But these piecemeal accounts of consequential leadership practices are difficult to use in thinking about how your own leadership might need to change or what experiences might be helpful to others in improving the quality of their leadership. The intellectual "glue" provided by a formal model helps with both of those challenges. So the purpose of this and the next chapter is to describe a school-specific model of transformational leadership. This model has been informed by many years of research in schools aimed at developing a contextually sensitive account of successful school leadership as well as exploring its influence on a number of organizational and student outcomes, including teacher emotions (e.g., Leithwood & Jantzi, 2005; Leithwood, Jantzi, & Steinbach, 1999).

Part of this description includes a demonstration of just how pervasive are the practices associated with our education-specific model of transformational leadership in other accounts of leadership both inside and outside of schools. Transformational practices are compared with practices found in the most fully researched model of instructional leadership (Hallinger, 2003), for example, as well as a recent and widely disseminated meta-analysis of school leadership practices influencing student learning (Marzano, Waters, and McNulty, 2005). Selected excerpts from interviews with teachers and principals were collected as part of our Wallace Foundation-funded study (Leithwood, Louis, Anderson, and Wahlstrom, 2004), a federally funded Canadian study of teacher emotions related to their experiences with leaders, and a study of the emotions of educational leadership (Beatty, 2002,[8] 2005, 2007a).

Lists of things such as leadership practices can be pretty forgettable and not very meaningful, unless some underlying idea is holding them together. One of the great advantages of leadership *theories* is

---

8. In Beatty's doctoral thesis (winner of the CASEA Thomas B. Greenfield Dissertation of the Year in Canada award), the teacher interview data that related to their experience with leaders were provided by a project titled *The Emotions of Teaching and Educational Change,* funded by the Social Science and Humanities Research Council of Canada as Grant No. 418699; the leader data were collected with the support of the University of Waikato, New Zealand.

that they possess a conceptual glue almost entirely missing from, for example, the many lists of leadership standards now so popular in policy circles or the lengthy lists of functions and responsibilities such as those described by Marzano et al. (2005). Theoretical glue offers a framework within which to consider how and why things work as they do and so builds connections and meaning.

The glue that holds transformational leadership practices together might be drawn from many sources, since the practices themselves reflect many elements of existing leadership theory. Chapter 1 briefly touched on transformational leadership theory, for example. But we offer a different type of theoretical glue at this point, glue that aims to explain why each of the main categories of practices in our conception of transformational leadership is important to exercise if leaders are to have a substantial and positive impact on teacher emotions and students' learning.

The extent to which educational policies and other reform efforts improve what students learn eventually depends on their consequences for what teachers do. And what teachers do, according to a particularly useful model for explaining workplace performance (O'Day, 1996; Rowan, 1996) is a function of their motivations, abilities, and the situations in which they work. For those of you who appreciate such things, the model is sometimes expressed as a mathematical function:

$$P = f(a, m, s)$$

where

P = teacher performance

a = teacher ability

m = teacher motivation

s = the setting in which teachers work

Relationships among the variables in this model are considered to be interdependent. This means two things. It means that each variable has an effect on the remaining two (for example, aspects of teachers' work environments are significant influences on their motivations). It also means that changes in all three variables need to happen in concert or performance will not change much. For example, neither high ability and low motivation, nor high motivation and low ability, foster high levels of teacher performance; neither does high ability and high motivation in a dysfunctional work environment. Furthermore, a dysfunctional work setting will likely depress initially high levels of both ability and motivation.

The implications for leadership practice in this account of workplace performance are twofold. First, leaders need to engage in practices with the potential to improve all elements in the model. The second implication is that leaders will need to engage in those practices more or less simultaneously; the overall goal of successful leadership is to improve the condition of all three variables. And to do this, leaders need to engage in four sets of practices described in this and the next chapter. This chapter describes practices classified as "Setting Directions" (primarily a motivational function, the m in the mathematical function) and "Developing People" (concerned with strengthening organizational members' abilities, the a in the function). The next chapter describes leadership practices classified as "Managing the Instructional Program" and "Redesigning the Organization" (the s in the function), both largely aimed at creating and refining settings or situations conducive to productive work by teachers and students.

To be clear, leaders have many things to worry about, teacher emotions being just one, albeit a critical one. So it is virtually impossible for a leader to consider separately and independently how to address each of these many issues. Instead, success depends on enacting a coherent set of practices that accomplishes many things at the same time. Building a shared vision with staff, for example, has its primary effects on staff motivation. But it also directs teachers' attention to the capacities they will need to develop, creates a framework for resource allocation in the school, sends a message to parents about what they can expect from their school, etc.

The transformational approach to leadership described in this and the next chapter, then, contribute a great deal to the emotional climate in the school—as well as many more outcomes. That multifaceted impact is one of its most important attributes.

SETTING DIRECTIONS

This category of practices carries the bulk of the effort to motivate leaders' colleagues (Hallinger & Heck, 1998). It is about the establishment of "moral purpose" (Fullan, 2003; Hargreaves & Fink, 2006) as a basic stimulant for one's work. Most theories of motivation, as Chapter 6 explained, argue that people are motivated to accomplish personally important goals for themselves. Such goals are among the four sources of motivation in Bandura's theory of human motivation (1986), for example.

Three more specific sets of practices are included in this category, all of which are aimed at bringing a focus to both the individual and collective work of staff in the school or district. Carried out skillfully, these practices become foundational sources of motivation and inspiration for the work of staff.

Building a Shared Vision

Building shared visions of the organization's future is a fundamental task included in both transformational and charismatic leadership models. Bass's (1985) "inspirational motivation" is encompassed in this practice, a dimension that Podsakoff, MacKenzie, Moorman, & Fetter (1990) defined as leadership behavior "aimed at identifying new opportunities for his or her unit . . . and developing, articulating, and inspiring others with his or her vision of the future" (p. 112). Silins and Mulford (2002) found positive and significant effects for students of a shared and monitored mission. Harris and Chapman's (2002) small-scale qualitative study of effective leadership in schools in England facing challenging circumstances reaffirmed previous research on successful schools:

> Of central importance . . . was the cooperation and alignment of others to [the leader's] set of values and vision. . . . Through a variety of symbolic gestures and actions, they were successful at realigning both staff and pupils to their particular vision. (p. 6)

Locke (2002) argued that formulating a vision for the organization is one of eight core tasks for senior leaders and a key mechanism for achieving integration or alignment of activities within the organization; that is, tying all the processes together so that they are not only consistent with one another but actively support one another. After Locke, we include as part of vision building the establishment of core organizational values. Core values specify the means by which the vision is to be accomplished.

Principals' own descriptions of their vision-building work help us to appreciate this dimension of leadership better. So here is what three principals interviewed during our Wallace Foundation project had to say:

> Well, my vision is that all kids are capable of learning and that we will do all that we can to help each one of them achieve that goal, regardless of where they come from.
>
> We will first create the vision [for programs that meet the students' needs] here, go to our staff, or vice versa. From there, I will then take it and bounce it off the curriculum director, and then we'll come back, meet with the department, and put our heads together to look at all different angles to it.
>
> It has been rather difficult just because [the teachers in this school] ... are from four different buildings and they've had different leadership. This group started this way, and that group started this way. So it is just really talking and getting to know them more on a personal level and really listening to them. Then I am able to start letting them know things that I feel and see that are important and so then they eventually tie into that.

As you will have noticed, the first principal spoke about the content of her own vision, while the second and third talked about the process of vision building; the third also mentioned the importance of spending time talking and getting to know teachers on a personal level and really listening to them. Beatty's research tells us that this is a highly valued leadership practice, especially the listening and personal connecting. When teachers in her study believed that the leader not only respected their contributions but also cared about their ideas and their personal well-being, they were loyal to those leaders and would do almost anything for them. The importance of this emotionally grounded connectedness with leaders is highly consistent with the rest of what we know about teachers' working conditions and, for that matter, from other work that Beatty has done with leaders around the world, about leaders' working conditions, too! The importance of a relational connection between leaders and teachers can hardly be overstated.

Without this deep listening by teachers and leaders about others' perspectives, their differing professional priorities can interfere with their emotional understanding of each other and the quality of their professional relationships. The following excerpt from a participant in the Beatty study illustrates the danger when leaders and teachers don't connect about their core purposes and come to appreciate and respect the differences in their respective goals:

> I think that many administrators are too concerned about the way they appear to the community, and by appearances; I mean physical appearances, involvement with police.... It's like an image thing, and I don't think that that's a school administrator's job necessarily. I think that the way the school truly runs and what the kids are getting out of it and how we... how our kids grow up in our school and what they accomplish is far more important than the way the outside of the building looks, the way the people look to the parents, the way we look to the Board.

With open discussion and genuine sharing of ideas and concerns, the diversity of perspectives and the place for both leaders' and teachers' goals within the whole can be appreciated and understood. This kind of bridge building toward shared goals is key to collective growth and school transformation. The impact principals can have on the building of a shared vision for the school is often meted out in daily, seemingly minor interactions. But the influence of these minor interactions accumulates over time. For teachers, feelings of being respected, personally valued, and professionally supported are critical:

> I find the current principal to be so cooperative and so genuine. No matter what you do with ____, you feel good about it.... He's really helpful.
>
> We have a wonderful principal. He is supportive of anything that you say.... My positive interactions would be with him on a day-to-day basis.
>
> Our VP is very supportive, and I think it is the ability to go in and see her and not feel that we're interrupting.... Every time that I go to see her, I always feel that my concern is an important one.... I have a lot of respect for that... very reinforcing because I feel I'm being listened to.

Fostering the Acceptance of Group Goals

While visions can be inspiring, both motivation and action require some agreement on the more immediate goals to be accomplished in order to move toward fulfilling the vision (Anderman & Wolters, 2006). Building on this understanding, this set of practices aims not only to identify important goals for the organization but to do so in such a way that individual members come to include the organization's goals among their own. Unless this happens, the organization's goals have no motivational value. So leaders can productively spend a lot of time on this set of practices. This set of practices includes leader relationship behaviors "aimed at promoting cooperation among [teachers] and getting them to work together toward a common goal" (Podsakoff et al., 1990, p. 112); giving short shrift to this idea misses the point entirely. Leaders in the Beatty (2002) study found that open discussion and frank consideration of shared goals and vision could be among the most exciting and satisfying work that they did, even though it was emotionally challenging in the beginning. Leaders need to exercise the courage to open up discussion, so that all voices are heard and all perspectives acknowledged. Studies are beginning to suggest that leadership development programs that address the emotional challenges leaders face are making a significant difference in the way leaders conceptualize and approach their work with teachers (Beatty, 2006).

In district and school settings, strategic and improvement planning processes are among the more explicit contexts in which these goal-setting leadership practices can occur. This seemingly rational planning process cannot be effected without attention to the importance of emotions. Two principals we interviewed had this to say about goal setting practices in their schools:

We do goal setting as a vertical team and share that with our site-based improvement committee, which is parents and administrators and teachers and outside people coming in, and then they vote on the goals, and they help form the goals for our school. And the vertical teams play a large role in that, in preparing the goals.

We've set our goal [for the number of students achieving at the required level] at 80%. "Eighty percent?" [some teachers said] "You're insane. Fifty

> *percent is more realistic. We know these kids. . . . You gotta get real!" And*
> *so I said to them, "You know, there could be some problems here, because*
> *we gotta be shoulder-to-shoulder. I'm gonna be honest with you. Me say-*
> *ing 80%—here's what I'm really saying: I'm willing to give up on 20%. And*
> *I have a hard time living with that. I have to look in the mirror every morn-*
> *ing when I shave, and I don't like myself when I think I'm giving up on*
> *20%. . . . That's an expression of my confidence in the profession and in*
> *you. How can you be insulted?"*

One of our teacher interviewees spoke about the importance of principals being actively engaged in the kind of follow-up in the school required for this leadership practice to make a difference. She said

> *[The school administrators'] presence is another big thing. Not just sitting*
> *in the office, seeing their presence and the students seeing their presence*
> *out and about, dropping in. . . . If everybody is on the same track and in*
> *the same boat and you are all going the same place, that works. If a*
> *teacher says they are not going to do it or that isn't going to work, that*
> *causes a lot of discord among the staff, because one bad apple, as they*
> *say, can spoil the whole bunch. I don't see that happening because of the*
> *administration.*

Dialogue between teachers and leaders needs to occur in a relationally safe space in which their actual perceptions can be shared openly and their new knowledge of each other and plans about how they will proceed together can be agreed upon. Without this dialogue, teachers regularly pay lip service to leaders' goals and then go their own way in the classroom. Not only follow-up but also active engagement in respectful, candid, two-way communication is essential.

A principal from one of Beatty's studies (2005) described how satisfying this shared vision building and goal setting can be. This principal spoke of taking the chance of letting go of control and asking open-ended questions in search of shared goals for the school's future. Looking back brought to her mind memories of an exciting collaboration with teachers. Reflecting on an open-ended, creative planning session where there was ambiguity and a sharing of "burning issues," this U.K. principal recalled the emotional intensity:

> *My aim is toward a learning organization ... where children and adults all want to learn more ... and that definitely includes me! ... This is the part of the job I love, the strategic plans, making it all happen.*

Inviting authentic encounters requires a different kind of courage, a counterintuitive awareness of the self-limiting cultural pressure not to risk loss of control. Entering ambiguous territory by asking open-ended questions, for instance, can be emotionally frightening and threatening for leaders. Those who dare to engage in this somewhat uncertain and sometimes stressful openness can serve the needs of the school while, at the same time, affirming the individuals within it. Here is a description of just such an occasion that yielded inspiring results:

> *The vision, direction, and clarity are the three most essential starting points to getting the leadership right, but it's risky! If you want your staff to follow— not follow but be part of it (metaphorically "buy a ticket"), you have to ask open questions about direction and the way to go. We have a "Vision Day" every four years. A training day given over to EVERYONE. All the staff and Governors are invited. On the first day, we explored learning styles, worked in cross-responsibility groups to find out the burning issues for addressing. ... Together we informed our mission statement. Four years on, we revisited the statement to see if it still rang true. It was tweaked and reapproved. How did I feel? An absolute sense of elation when the things that were hot for me were also the hot issues for them, should I say OUR hot issues. And all that from open questions. ... We live the model everyday.*

Having the courage to take creative risks is as much of an issue for leaders as for teachers. Risking with staff can be threatening. In this case, the rewards were exhilarating. However, while the ability to find sufficient security for bold leadership may be necessary for "getting it right," the courage to make countercultural and emotionally counterintuitive moves also requires a depth of self-awareness that may not be supported by the culture typical of educational administration. Leaders need ways of creating shared understandings *with* teachers. To develop this ability, alternative support systems, such as those provided through online, anonymous discussion groups and small peer discussion and study groups of leaders, are useful. They help leaders make the shift from devaluing teacher emotions to engaging with teachers in emotional meaning making (Beatty, 2002).

Creative collaborations can inspire hope for possibilities, especially when personal needs, professional interests, and organizational goals coalesce (Beatty, 2000b). These conditions involve risk and reward: the excitement of creating new opportunities together and the emotionally powerful and culturally regenerative shared experience of "flow" (Csikzentmihalyi, 1990). The notion of a culture of relatedness echoes Margolis's (1998) associations among self, ethics, and emotions and Sergiovanni's (1992) concepts of moral leadership in a community of connectedness. A shared sense of moral purpose can evoke feelings of love and deep satisfaction that strengthen and embolden the entire learning community.

Demonstrating High Performance Expectations

This set of leadership practices is included as part of "Direction Setting" because it is closely aligned with goals. While high performance expectations do not define the substance of organizational goals, they demonstrate the leader's values and, as Podsakoff et al. (1990) explained, "the leader's expectations of excellence, quality, and/or high performance"(p. 112) in the achievement of those goals. Demonstrating such expectations is a key practice in virtually all conceptions of transformational and charismatic leadership. Two of our interviewed principals spoke of their expectations in these words:

> I have high expectations for myself, and I, in turn, articulate that to my staff. I want it to be a safe, friendly, caring environment where kids will do their absolute best.

> The number one focus here is student success. It is all about the kids and that we work hard. We appreciate one another, and I want everybody to be treated with courtesy and respect.... We work hard, and I have high expectations. I expect the students and everyone else to meet those expectations and go above them. So it is not going to be easy.

A principal in Beatty's study had also found that "the desire for high standards can produce teamwork and develop a cooperative ethos in school." These high expectations, of course, need to be visible to staff and students. When they are, their impact is palpable, as this observation from one of our teacher interviewees illustrates:

> One thing is that we have what is called the "no excuses policy" for the year. There is no excuse for you not doing your best effort, whether you are staff, whether you are a student, whether you're a parent, or whatever. We are trying to focus on that.

DEVELOPING PEOPLE

The three sets of practices in this category (individualized support, intellectual stimulation, and modeling) make a significant contribution to staff motivation. Their primary aim is capacity building, however. This involves building not only the knowledge and skill staff need to accomplish organizational goals but also their commitment and resilience and the disposition to persist in applying that knowledge and skill (Harris & Chapman, 2002). Individual teacher efficacy is arguably critical to these dispositions, and it is a third source of motivation in Bandura's (1986) model. People are motivated by what they are good at. And *mastery experiences,* according to Bandura, are the most powerful sources of efficacy, as we discussed in some detail in Chapter 4. So building capacity that leads to a sense of mastery is highly motivational, as well. In Beatty's study of Ontario teachers' experiences with leaders, the connection between leaders' attitudes to teachers and teachers' attitudes to themselves and their work was clear:

> [T]he thing is they believe in the teacher....And I thought that had a really good positive impact on me. And this is why you do more....But then you have the principal that you feel you're limited, or you feel that you have difficulty to work with...then it stops.

When teachers experience success, they develop positive self-efficacy, and as we have discussed in earlier chapters, leaders have a role to play in teachers' belief in their own capacity for development and openness to try new things. Explained a teacher interviewee,

> *That is the reason I am staying in the profession. Those are the things that motivate you to come back the next day. If you are successful ... you will want to try something else. You won't be afraid ... because the likelihood of being successful will continue. There are people watching and telling you that you are doing a good job.*

Leaders are emotionally significant "others" in teachers' lives and affect a large part of teachers' disposition to be open to new ideas and new practices. Another teacher from the same study recalled how her principal conveyed his understanding of her work:

> *I remember one principal. ... In his own quiet way, he was able to acknowledge what you were doing. There was a pervasive feeling in that school that he knew what you were about. He did it in very small ways. It could be a smile. It could be a note in your mailbox. It could be a chat over coffee. Somehow he conveyed it. He was very professional.*

When teachers have their talents and potential acknowledged by their leaders, they adjust their professional sights and feel encouraged to develop. Sometimes leaders have potentially career-altering impacts on teachers, as in the following comment:

> *We had to have a meeting with the vice principal and the principal to discuss our portfolios. One of the aims is long-range goals and the vice principal said to me, "Wow, now that you're in Special Ed maybe you'll be going on looking for a resource position." And I said, "Oh, I don't think so." And she said, "Don't you be so sure, I think you would do a good job at that. ..." And I thought how nice for her to have that confidence in me that I don't have in myself ... it really made me feel good.*

Conversely, as leaders interact with teachers, or ignore them, they can also have damaging effects. Evidence of this was pervasive across the negative stories told by the 50 teachers in Beatty's study.

Providing Individualized Support and Consideration

Bass and Avolio (1994) included, as part of this dimension, "knowing your followers' needs and raising them to more mature levels . . . [sometimes through] the use of delegation to provide opportunities for each follower to self-actualize and to attain higher standards of moral development" (p. 64). This set of behaviors, claimed Podsakoff et al. (1990), should communicate a leader's respect for colleagues and concerns about their personal feelings and needs (emotional understanding and support). This set of practices is common to all of the early two-dimensional models of leadership (Ohio State, Contingency theory, and Situational Leadership theory) that include task orientation and *consideration for people*. Encompassed by this set of practices are the "supporting" and "recognizing and rewarding" managerial behaviors associated with Yukl's (1989) Multiple Linkage model, as well as Hallinger's (2003) model of instructional leadership and the Waters, Marzano, & McNulty (2003) meta-analysis. This set of leadership behaviors has likely attracted more leadership research outside of schools since the 1960s than any other.

Here are several principals talking about some of the work they do to support their colleagues:

> I try to do a lot of coaching, encouraging, making connections. I will try to focus more time on teachers who seem to be having some difficulty and will try to encourage them to try a particular strategy or probably just do more encouraging, supporting, problem solving.
>
> We [the school leaders] do about an hour, an hour and a half, four times a year, sitting down and talking with each individual teacher and learning about what's going on in their classroom. . . . It also lets them know how much we support what they're doing. . . . If they're really struggling, then we can sit down with them even further and try to assist them in any way that we can.

A leader from Beatty's study expressed a similar commitment to and delight in teacher development:

> *Teachers are marvelous creatures. With my staff I feel the same. They achieve terrific things, especially if they are treated as trained, sensible adults who want to do a good job. It's important to let them get on with it. Giving a responsibility to a budding young teacher and seeing him or her thrive and grow is just as satisfying and good fun as seeing students learn.*

Supportive and considerate practices, of the sort described by these three principals, have important consequences for the way teachers feel about their work. Comments by two of our teacher interviewees illustrate some of those feelings:

> *I love my principal. She pretty much supports everything that we do in our classroom. Even yesterday, I was out of my room and we had some difficulty with someone who was in the room, and that person ended up being asked to leave and my principal came in and took over my classroom for the rest of the day. I mean she's just that type of person.*
>
> *I mean, he comes to my class a lot, sees what I'm doing, goes in, saying, "You know, what's going on? What are we doing today?" He's actually come in, and we've actually team-taught a couple of times just—off-the-cuff he came in, and we have similar backgrounds, so he came in, and we were talking—I forget what the lesson was the one day—oh, it was about the elections, back in November.*

This kind of constructive interaction about teaching was highly valued by the teachers in Beatty's study. Conversely, omission of this kind of constructive interaction about teaching generated negative emotions among teachers and a perception of disconnection and disdain for the leader. No matter what leaders do or do not do in this regard, they will have an impact on teacher emotions—one way or the other:

There was a VP here years back. He always gave me really positive feedback. He would come into my class for five to ten minutes; later on when I would see him, he would say that whatever I was saying or teaching at that time "was really interesting." I don't get that from many administrators [now]. They just walk in and walk out.

In the past, quite a lot. So positive, there is no positive. . . . The [previous] principal would always give you positive feedback about your program, about what you are doing. This principal says nothing whatsoever. I don't even think she knows the children in this school.

Increases in the complexity and sheer quantity of principals' work responsibilities in recent years has encroached upon the time they feel they can afford to spend in connecting with teachers; this is the case not only about what teachers do for the school image but also their core purposes in teaching their students. This was a recurring theme among this teacher's recollections:

I think that there is recognition outside of the classroom in terms of extracurricular. You could be coaching a team, and the team does well. If you are the coach, then you get that recognition that you are doing well. I don't think there is enough of it in the classroom. Administration walks through the classroom all the time. I think that's great, but what I would like to see is for them to say, "You are doing a really darn good job. Every time I come in, the kids are interested, there are good dynamics occurring in the class, and they are busy doing things." I don't think there is enough of that. . . . I mean, I get a thank-you note for helping out on things that occur outside of the class. Within the class, it doesn't happen. If you asked staff, they would most likely say the same thing. It doesn't happen.

In many of today's schools, the accountability push has increased the focus on academic outcomes and improved instruction. This is helping leaders reorder their priorities, placing a renewed emphasis on classroom practices. However, the individual support teachers perceive they can expect from their leaders matters emotionally and thus impacts their effectiveness, as we have discussed throughout this book. One teacher put it this way:

> *They really should make it their business to find out what does truly go on in the classroom and ... somehow convey to you that they are aware. Even to this day, I realize that there are a lot of really super teachers out there who continue to do a really fine job all the time. You need the feedback.*

Offering Intellectual Stimulation

Behaviors in this dimension include encouraging colleagues to take intellectual risks, re-examine assumptions, look at their work from different perspectives, rethink how it can be performed (Avolio, 1994; Podsakoff et al., 1990), and otherwise "induc[e] ... employees to appreciate, dissect, ponder and discover what they would not otherwise discern ..." (Lowe, Kroeck, & Sivasubramaniam, 1996, pp. 415–416). Waters et al. (2003) and Marzano et al. (2005) included "challenging the status quo" among the practices contributing to leader effects on students.

This is where the leader's role in professional development is key, especially for leaders of schools in challenging circumstances (Day, Hadfield, & Harris, 1999); Gray, 2000; Harris & Chapman, 2002). However, this set of practices can take many forms—informal as well as formal. Leaders need not always do this job personally, either. They "simply" need to make sure it gets done by, for example, providing resources for teacher-identified professional development opportunities, designating and supporting a staff development position in the school, or encouraging teachers to visit other schools to learn about best practices elsewhere. This set of practices also reflects current understandings of learning as constructed, social, and situated. All models of transformational and charismatic leadership include this set of practices. A considerable amount of the educational literature assumes such practices on the part of school leaders, most notably the literature on instructional leadership, which places school leaders at the center of instructional improvement efforts in their schools (e.g., Day, Harris, Hadfield, Tolley, & Beresford, 2000; Hallinger, 2003; Southworth, 1998; Stein & Spillane, 2005).

Three of our principal interviewees described different facets of what it means to provide intellectual stimulation to their teaching colleagues:

> When there is something that is topical or that is innovative or that is controversial, I make sure that I get that to the staff and that we talk about it.
>
> Where it all comes back down from is really, how is that [instructional method] supported, like, researchwise? ... Do you have something that will support this method as being advantageous and successful for the kids?
>
> Building administrators have had the opportunity to receive much of the same professional development that our teachers were receiving. So that the same information, but also the same foundational pieces that teachers got, were being shared with us. What that has, I think, helped—at least again in my case—is that I could speak to teachers in language that they would understand. ... So the conversation has been more meaningful.

Comments by two of our teacher interviewees also help illustrate the range of ways in which leaders provide intellectual stimulation:

> When we pose an idea, they [the school leaders] ... say, "Well, let me hear about it. How are you going to do this, and how is that going to tie into this? How is this going to help the children?" It always goes back to how it is going to affect the children. How will the children grow in this? Will this make a difference?
>
> There's a whole section in the library that he [the principal] orders. He says, "I want you to read this book." There's always at least one copy of that book. He supplies articles about what's going on in the world. He really knows his stuff, too, and that helps out.

Providing an Appropriate Model

This category of practices entails "leading by example," a general set of practices associated with models of "authentic leadership" (Avolio & Gardner, 2005), demonstrating transparent decision making, confidence, optimism, hope, resilience, and consistency between words and deeds. Locke (2002) claimed that core values are established when leaders model such values in their own practices. Both Hallinger (2003) and Waters et al. (2003) noted the contribution to leader effects of maintaining high visibility in the school, a visibility associated with high-quality interactions with both staff and students. Harris and Chapman (2002) found that their successful headteachers "modeled behaviour that they considered desirable to achieve the school goals" (p. 6).

Also encompassed by this dimension is Bass's "idealized influence," a partial replacement for his original "charisma" dimension (1985). Avolio (1994) claimed that leaders exercise idealized influence when they serve as role models with the appropriate behaviors and attitudes that are required to build trust and respect in followers. Such modeling on the part of leaders "sets an example for employees to follow that is consistent with the values the leader espouses" (Podsakoff et al., 1990, p. 112).

Two principals spoke about their modeling efforts in these words:

What I try to do is model what I would like to happen.... If a teacher brings a student to me and they have a sarcastic or disgusted tone to them, I might try to turn that around a little bit and model something different, so that the teacher has some other way they can relate to the student but yet convey the message that what they did was inappropriate.

So I will model for the teacher. I will take the class over if necessary. I will work with a few students or a small group in the class.

One of our teacher interviewees offered a relatively nuanced view of the kind of modeling that would and would not be helpful from a principal:

So he's very good. His leadership—he's very hands-on.... But he's not hands-on to where he's meddling.... Because I've seen or heard people where hands-on has been counterproductive, where they micromanage. He doesn't do that. So his leadership is more by—he leads by example. He's always open to suggestions.

A teacher in the Beatty study connected her respect for her principal with the principal's focus on the children, a sign of their shared moral purpose:

[T]he best principal that I've ever been under... she really cares for the kids more than any other principal I've worked for. And this is really important to me.... She's always there. I really like her for being that way. So I can always kid with her and stuff as a result. The previous principal was nice. It's not that I didn't get along with him. He was like so many of them are, very political, very professional, and kept you at arm's length. And with him, just to get approval for a chocolate bar drive took me a month. I feel very comfortable with her. I respect what she does.

There is an old adage about people being more influenced by what you do than what you say. It is an adage that applies especially well to leaders.

CONCLUSION

The leadership practices described in this chapter are about purposes and people. They have a powerful influence on teachers' workplace motivations and their sense of efficacy—both individual and collective. These practices are also significant contributors to teachers' morale and job satisfaction when they provide teachers with a clearer sense of what they should be doing, thereby reducing an important source of unnecessary job complexity. A shared vision helps direct and motivate people's attention and align people's actions around the same goals. To the extent that a shared vision is based on fundamental values that are also widely shared, it increases commitment to work and provides opportunities for people to experience deeper levels of satisfaction in their work.

The specific leadership practices we associated with Developing People are primarily intended to build teachers' knowledge and skills. But the theoretical explanations we have explored in this chapter make evident the close relationship between a person's actual capacities, their beliefs about those capacities, and both their motivation and sense of efficacy. So building teacher abilities is an all-purpose leadership function. It transcends the useful but finally artificial constructs that social scientists have created in their efforts to understand what makes people tick. Creating shared purposes serves to guide our choice of the abilities we help our colleagues acquire and provides them with a meaningful explanation for why acquiring those capacities is important.

CHAPTER EIGHT

Leading With Teacher Emotions in Mind

Redesigning the Organization and Managing the Instructional Program

The two broad categories of leadership practice described in this chapter—"redesigning the organization" and "managing the instructional program"—address the *s*—the situation, or working conditions, variable in our equation predicting teacher performance described in Chapter 7. Little is to be gained by increasing teachers' motivations and abilities if working conditions will not allow their effective application. In Bandura's (1986) model of human motivation, beliefs about the situation in which one finds oneself are a key source of motivation; people are motivated when they believe the circumstances in which they find themselves are conducive to accomplishing the goals they hold to be personally important.

REDESIGNING THE ORGANIZATION

Our previous accounts of this category of leadership behavior included specific practices aimed at building collaborative cultures, providing structures to allow for collaboration, establishing productive relationships with parents and the wider community, and connecting the organization to the wider environment. These remain important elements of a successful leader's repertoire. But the evidence about teacher emotions examined in earlier chapters indicates that there is a great deal more than this upon which leaders should focus their efforts to improve working conditions. So this section of the chapter significantly extends earlier accounts of successful leaders' organizational redesign efforts by synthesizing the productive working conditions that surfaced in earlier chapters.

This summary of emotionally important working conditions is organized into four categories: classroom-level working conditions, schoolwide working conditions, district working conditions, and conditions created by the wider environment.

Classroom-Level Working Conditions

At the classroom level, evidence suggests that both the volume and complexity of teachers' workloads have important consequences.

Workload Volume. During the school year, teachers work an average of 50–53 hours per week doing a long list of tasks. About half of that time is devoted to actual classroom instruction. One middle school teacher we interviewed had this to say about her workload:

> I have a big workload. I have four preps and four different classes to teach, so that's really weighing on me this year. In the past, I have had . . . mostly three preps, which is still more than you get at high school . . . so I know that's a problem with some of the people in the school.

Teachers' overall attitude about the volume of their work depends on their perceptions of five more specific features of their environments. Reduced morale and commitment to their school, along with increased feelings of stress, are likely when teachers perceive their workload to be unfair in comparison with the work of other teachers in their own school or across the district. (The teacher quoted above, for example, compared her preparation load unfavorably with the preparation load of high school teachers, as she understood it.) These negative emotions are also engendered when teachers consider the overall number of pupils for which they are responsible to be excessive (four classes clearly seemed excessive to our middle school interviewee). Teachers' commitment and stress are negatively influenced, as well, by class sizes that are perceived to make unreasonable demands on the time required for preparation and marking and to erode the opportunities for providing differentiated instruction for students.

Excessive paperwork (filling in forms, collecting information for others, etc.) and the burden of such nonteaching demands as hall monitoring, bus duty, and lunchroom supervision add to teachers' feelings of stress, reducing their morale and commitment to the school and increasing the likelihood of seriously considering moving on to another school or another line of work.

Workload Complexity. The complexity of their work, as teachers' perceive it, influences the same emotions as does workload volume. Job satisfaction also is eroded by teachers' perceptions of an excessively complex teaching assignment. Perceptions of excessive complexity arise when teachers are required to teach in areas for which they are not certified or otherwise prepared: one of our first-year middle school interviewees described her feelings about this issue as follows:

> I was hired to teach language arts, and it was not communicated to me that there would be other classes I'd be responsible for teaching. I would never say I'm competent to teach the [Spanish] class. I would never have identified myself as that. . . . Definitely that caused some tension at the beginning of the school year. . . . I probably wouldn't have taken this job had I known that. I had other job offers that were just social studies or just language arts—I'm endorsed in both. So that set a bad tone, probably for the year.

Another teacher explained the effects on the complexity of her work of the relatively prescribed nature of the curriculum she is expected to teach:

Well, I just know that we were under a lot of pressure to be cookie-cutter teachers that all do the same thing because it is also very time limited. I mean, if you had 40 minutes for your writing block and of that, you were to take 10 minutes to do a minilesson in which you taught a language arts skill, but you stopped at the end of that 10 minutes and then you went into your writing time where you conferenced with the kids and they would write. Well, if they didn't get it in that 10 minutes, that was it. . . . I can't teach like that. . . . You know everybody was like, "Why are they doing this? This isn't working."

Complexity also increases for teachers when their students achieve relatively poorly and when they are uncooperative. Describing her feelings about uncooperative student behavior, one junior high school teacher we interviewed said about her current cohort:

These kids came in, and I felt like they dropped a bomb in my classroom. It was really difficult.

Complexity is perceived to be increasingly manageable, however, when teachers are given a significant degree of autonomy over classroom decisions. This allows them to do the job the best way they know how. Illustrating the negative emotions arising when there is little autonomy, one of our eighth-grade teacher interviewees explained:

Sometimes you get some frustrations from the teachers that people are second-guessing them and telling them what to do, almost like they want to create a curriculum that views teaching as more of something that can just be read off and done, not necessarily as an art or a skill. That has created some significant frustrations that I have had to deal with in trying to let people know that they are still valued and that their opinions still matter and that they still make a difference in the classroom.

Manageability also is increased by an atmosphere throughout the school that encourages learning and when instructional resources are readily available.

School-Level Working Conditions

Four sets of school-level working conditions have a significant influence on teacher emotions—school cultures, school structures, relations with the community, and the school's standard operating procedures.

School Cultures. School culture has significant effects on all seven of the emotion sets we have examined. Increasingly positive contributions are made to the emotional lives of teachers by school cultures in which

- the goals for teachers' work are clear, explicit, and shared;
- there is little conflict in teachers' minds about what they are expected to do;
- the atmosphere in the school is generally positive and friendly;
- student indiscipline is under control; and
- collaboration among teachers is encouraged.

Teachers also thrive when the cultures of their schools value and support their safety and the safety of their students and when there are high expectations for students with a strong academic "press" evident to students and teachers across the school. School cultures that help teachers to find their work meaningful (e.g., clear and morally inspiring goals) also have a positive influence on teachers' affective dispositions.

School Structures. The primary purpose for school structures is to make possible the development and maintenance of cultures that support the work of teachers and the learning of students. Not all of the structures about which our review of research provided evidence are alterable, at least not easily or in the short term, however. This is the case for school size and location, in particular. Evidence does suggest that the emotions and work of teachers are most likely to thrive in small schools and in suburban rather than urban locations. Not much can be done about school size or location. However, "schools-within-schools" is currently a popular response to large school structures, and foundation support for the creation of small high schools has provided a major stimulus for action on this matter.

All other structural attributes of schools associated with teacher emotions are potentially quite malleable, however, and can easily outweigh the negative effects of larger school sizes and urban locations. Positive contributions to teacher emotions and their classroom practices are associated with structures, such as common planning times, that provide teachers opportunities to collaborate with one another. Explaining why she felt so positive about her working conditions, for example, one of our third-grade teacher interviewees said the following:

> There is a lot of sharing of ideas. I work with a first-grade teacher also, and we bring our students together once a week to direct activities and read with the first graders, and so there is collaboration between grade levels so you can go in very comfortably.

Positive emotions are stimulated by opportunities to work in small teams, prepare adequately for classroom instruction, and access ongoing professional development. Participation in school-level decisions contributes to a positive emotional climate, but the participation must be authentic to have this effect. A middle school teacher explained how she felt when participation was not authentic:

> I also feel as far as the leadership goes, there have been some things that we've met about, and had committees about, and things have been decided that had nothing to do with the outcome of the committee. And that's been really hard to take. Because you feel like you have a part in this decision-making thing, and then you really don't. And it was a waste of time.... At the district level, I feel that people are hand-picked who are going to go the direction that the administration or the district wants.... It's hard, when you know you have an opposing opinion from the person who's going to these district meetings and they're representing your school.

Physical facilities that permit teachers to use the types of instruction they judge to be most effective increase teachers' engagement in their schools and desire to remain in the profession, as do well-developed and stable programs on which to build when new challenges present themselves.

Community Relations. A third set of school-level conditions, community relations, influences teachers' job satisfaction as well as engagement—the probability of remaining in the school and the profession. Positive contributions to these emotions occur when the reputation of the school in the local community is positive and when parents and the wider community provide considerable support for the efforts and directions of the school. How much support is enough? One teacher we interviewed spoke to this question:

> In this small town, we have good support. There are some that don't. You know you are going to find that anywhere. ... I would say that 75% of my parents are excellent in their support for what their child is learning.

On the other hand, it doesn't seem to take many unsupportive parents to make life stressful for some teachers. One of our teachers explained,

> I am having a hard time this year with some parents. ... Their expectations on a teacher, I feel, are unrealistic. Their students are not doing their part, and the parent is looking to blame the teacher. That's been a real hard one.

So leaders need to be seen by teachers to be involved in helping to defuse unrealistic parental expectations on their behalf.

School Operating Procedures. Finally, there are three working conditions at the school level that, as a group, influence teachers' sense of individual and collective efficacy as well their job satisfaction and organizational commitment. These include quality of communication, school improvement planning, and regular feedback. We use the term *standard operating procedures* to encompass all three.

Although quality of communication seems an obviously important matter with which leaders must concern themselves, consider the fuller story told to us by a first-year middle school teacher assigned to teach outside her specialty:

The principal's never been in my classroom. Which I guess is neither here nor there in terms of how I feel about my teaching in the classroom, my relationships with the kids. But I realize that she, nonetheless, has a lot of influence of what could or could not happen in terms of like classes that I teach. She's the one who determines which classes I teach. . . . I was hired to teach language arts, and it was not communicated to me that there would be other classes I'd be responsible for teaching. So I got hired last May, didn't talk to [the principal] all summer, got to school in August thinking, great, I'm teaching language arts. And then just happened to see on the schedule, [teacher's name] also teaching social studies and reading and Spanish. And I was like, what? And it was never communicated to me. To this day it's never been, ever, never, ever sat down and talked to you like, [teacher's name], we kind of have these other classes we're interested in you teaching. Do you feel comfortable with that? Can we talk about what that will look like? Can we get you curriculum help? Can we give you mentor teachers? It was kind of like, well, she'll figure it out.

And we wonder why so many new teachers don't survive!

One of our Ontario studies revealed the emotional significance to teachers of face-to-face communication with leaders. Overrepresented in negative emotional experiences were occasions of lack of communication altogether and one-way communication, while overrepresented in positive emotional experiences were occasions of engaged, two-way communications. Among the 100 teacher accounts about school leaders, incidents involving school operating procedures were recalled only in connection with negative emotional memories. Leaders can reduce the negative emotions of teachers by giving consideration to their concerns and, ideally, consulting with teachers in advance. Also influencing teacher efficacy, satisfaction, and commitment is the match between the school's plans for improvement and teachers' views of what the school's priorities should be. Teachers exhibit consternation and even disgust at an apparent dissonance between a leader's preoccupation with the image of the school and teachers' abiding focus on what goes on in classrooms. Bridging perceptions about priorities by discussing them openly with teachers is a challenge to which successful leaders rise.

Evidence also points to the value of providing regular feedback to school working groups and individual teachers about the focus and quality of their progress. In particular, teachers value interactions with their leaders about core purposes and how best to work with children in their classrooms. In the Ontario study mentioned above, teachers strongly lamented the lack of leaders' awareness of their classroom work. Across the 100 stories told by these teachers, both positive and negative, occasions where leaders had connected with their teachers about their teaching were all but nonexistent. The implication for leaders is clear. Teachers value being known and recognized by their leaders, not only for their extracurricular contributions and assistance in managing the external image of the school but especially for their teaching.

Most of the school-level working conditions depend on skillful school-level leadership; improving them does not require significant new money.

District Working Conditions

Districts have significant, if not primary, "control" over a small number of working conditions about which teachers feel strongly, including teachers' professional development opportunities, salaries, and the pace of change. District size turns out to be of some significance for teachers, as well. These conditions influence teachers' individual efficacy, job satisfaction, organizational commitment, stress, and morale.

Professional Development. Considerable variation across districts seems likely in teachers' access to meaningful professional development, and there is good reason to believe that significant improvement is called for in many districts. For example, teachers in Dibbon's (2004) study indicated that access to inservice opportunities for new programs they were asked to teach was

> inappropriately timed, inadequate or non-existent. Two thirds of the teachers in this study had one day or less and 21% with a new course indicated that they had no inservice at all. (p. 28)

Along the same lines, one teacher we interviewed described her experiences with a mentoring program, the product of good intentions and poor implementation, as follows:

> When I first came, there was a mentoring program. But the person who was my mentor was a home-and-careers teacher who is on the first floor of the building on the opposite end. You know, and her style is completely different from mine, and really I had taught for five years and that just really was not helpful. And then they had teacher meetings for new teachers, but it was on Fridays and we are so overburdened. They make you do all these—they are so mean to their teachers—there is so much they make you do in this district with portfolios and looking for everything, and to give us another Friday meeting where they would say things like, "Oh, you have to take some time for yourself." You know, we were almost in tears. So that was really kind of hard. I think sometimes they really mean to support the new teachers, but instead—new teachers—I think they have had over 50% turnover since I have started here.

Teacher Salaries. Typically much more under district rather than school control, teacher salaries have significant effects on teachers' internal states, in spite of the fact that teachers are among the most altruistic of occupational groups. Salaries have a particularly significant impact on teachers' feelings when they are noticeably lower than teachers' salaries in nearby districts.

Pace of Change. Districts are a frequent source of change—new guidelines, new standards, new programs, new forms of student assessment, and the like. Both the nature and speed of such change can become a significant source of stress for teachers. This is the case when changes are determined with little teacher consultation and when they actually fly in the face of what teachers believe should be the priorities.

Teachers also experience dysfunctional levels of stress when they believe the timetable for implementing district changes is unrealistically short. Extra time of teachers is also required by these changes, time to make appropriate adaptations as well as to implement them well in the classroom. Dibbon's (2004) study in the Canadian province of Newfoundland and Labrador found, for example, that almost one-third of teachers identified "new programs and curricula" as a major workload issue; 47% of teachers in this study were teaching one new course, 25% two new courses, and 10% three new courses. Each new course, these teachers estimated, required in excess of one extra hour of preparation each week on top of an average 52-hour work week.

Size. Finally, large district (as with class and school) structures are typically less able to provide such helpful conditions of work for teachers as a district wide sense of community and differentiated allocation of resources in support of unique classroom and school improvement efforts.

District level leaders could significantly enhance teachers' working conditions by slowing down the pace of change and by ensuring that teachers have access to meaningful professional development to assist with necessary changes.

Conditions in the External Environment

The "external environment" includes state/provincial departments of education and wider social forces.

Departments of Education. Like districts, state or provincial governments and their education departments are often sources of substantial change through, for example, their enactment of new policies and guidelines. Teachers' job satisfaction, organizational commitment, and continuing engagement in the school or profession are seriously eroded when the pace of these changes seems too rapid, when they demand extra time from teachers both to learn about and to implement them, and when they seem erratic or unresponsive to what teachers believe are the real needs of schools and students. One of the fifth-grade teachers we interviewed expressed her frustration this way:

As a district, we had a great curriculum going. It was reviewed every several, you know, every couple of years we'd review it. We'd add to it, we'd take parts of it out, we'd change it. We were already doing what we were supposed to be doing. We have the state standards coming in now, and it's test, test, test, test, test, test. We can't get to a lot of the fun things we used to have. In the springtime, we used to study plants, and I would well, the third-grade teachers would all get together and we'd do a spring musical on ecology. We don't have time to do that anymore. We're too worried about the all this junk that we have to do [sound of pile of paper being picked up]. All of this stuff that we have to do.... It's just it's just mind-boggling, all the junk we have to do with all those numbers, when we're doing a great job anyway. [Name of state] schools have always been in the top 10 for achievement, or the testing proved it. So why do we have to keep proving it, you know? It just makes me angry.

Accountability-oriented policies also have been associated with teachers' intentions and decisions to leave the profession.

Wider Social Forces. These conditions include both the community's views of teaching and its status and how those views are portrayed in the media. Negative views and media portrayals significantly erode teachers' job satisfaction and increase the chances of their leaving the profession. Alternative employment opportunities also increase the chances of teachers' leaving the profession, although such opportunities are not equally available to all teachers.

School- and district-level leaders can improve teacher working conditions by integrating as many state initiatives as possible into district and school initiatives and pushing back on state initiatives that are disruptive for teachers who are working effectively to improve student learning. School and district leaders also have important roles to play in the wider community, in some cases ambassadorial and public relations roles. Usually, these roles entail leaders' educating the wider public about the important work of schools and the contributions of teachers to that work.

MANAGING THE INSTRUCTIONAL PROGRAM

The handful of specific practices included in this category of our transformational school leadership model are important because they help create organizational stability and strengthen the school's infrastructure. Such stability and infrastructure allow staff to be confident in getting on with the more complex parts of their jobs without having to worry about the organization getting in the way.

Staffing the Program

Although not touched on in most accounts of successful school leadership (e.g., Hallinger, 2003; Waters, Marzano, & McNulty, 2003), staffing has proved to be a key function of leaders engaged in school improvement. Finding teachers with the interest and capacity to further the school's efforts is the goal of this activity. Recruiting and retaining staff is a primary task of leading schools in challenging circumstances (Gray, 2000). As one of our principal interviewees explained,

> *I have tried to find individuals who are child centered. I look at my position as being able to have the talent to provide the appropriate resources so the teachers can do their jobs, but also helping me do mine, is having the right people on board with you. While we may not always be able to have a say on who comes in, I try to then help the people who need more guidance with the strong advocates I have here in my building. I have done a lot of maneuvering of teams. I have tried to hire individuals who can do a variety of things for us. If something doesn't work, I try a different format.*

Another principal illustrated his orientation to staffing as follows:

> *As a matter of fact, I will be hiring a new teacher. . . . So we have control over what our staff looks like. . . . So it is about hiring good people, but it is not always a guarantee. It is about keeping good people.*
>
> *[Success takes] strong administration and then believing in your staff, selecting the right staff members that have the same goals.*

Providing Instructional Support

This set of practices, included in both Hallinger's (2003) and Waters' et al. (2003) research on effective leadership includes "supervising and evaluating instruction"; coordinating the curriculum"; and providing resources in support of curriculum, instruction, and assessment activity. West, Ainscow, and Stanford (2005) indicated that, for leaders of schools in challenging contexts, focusing on teaching and learning is essential. This includes controlling behavior, boosting self-esteem, and talking and listening to pupils. It also may include urging pupils and teachers to place a strong emphasis on pupil achievement. Such an "academic climate" makes significant contributions to achievement (De Maeyer, Rymenans, Van Petegem, van der Bergh, & Rijlaarsdam, 2006). One of our principal interviewees spoke about this aspect of her leadership in this way:

> *Even though I think we are doing a great job, I think we can always do a better job. That is my focus: just preparing the kids as best we can, having a caring environment, and closing the achievement gap.*

Another principal said,

> *Oh, it has everything to do with our staff development. Because it is trying to create programs for kids that will improve or get achievement so that we can get them at a higher level. Part of it is having a fairly focused vision around student achievement. And that's just a nonnegotiable in all of our other school improvement efforts, as we've got to be having measurable results.*

From a teacher's perspective, instructional support also includes the provision of professional development, although we have located that leadership function within what we described earlier as Intellectual Stimulation.

> *Professional days are kind of up to the discretion of the principal in the building. . . . Or they'll say, "Hey, you need to go to this conference." They'll get you a sub, and they'll pay your mileage and meals and all that. So they're supportive of that.*

Monitoring School Activity

Waters et al. (2003) associated leadership's effects on students with leader monitoring and evaluating functions, especially those focused on student progress. Purposeful use of data was reported by West et al. (2005) to be a central explanation for effective leadership in failing schools. And Hallinger's (2003) instructional leadership model included a set of practices labeled "monitoring student progress." Monitoring operations and environment was one of Yukl's (1989) 11 effective managerial practices. And Gray (2000) reported that tracking student progress is a key task for leaders of schools in challenging circumstances.

One of our teachers described her principal's monitoring activities in this way:

> *She has given the teachers what are called relief days where . . . she has substitutes in our classrooms. We sit and we analyze the data that the kids have produced. She is really a data-driven person. That is one of the things I admire about her, because that is one of the things that I enjoy, too, is the data. The data is what you have to go by.*

Several principals also provided us with a glimpse of the type of monitoring that goes on in their schools:

> We use it [student performance data] in several ways. We will meet as a whole school with our teaching staff and work with our school improvement plan, where we have goals that we have established: math goals and language arts goals.... We talk about how we are accomplishing those goals. At the end of each year, we review that plan to see how we did that year.
>
> So we're seeing a progressing improvement in our assessments. That's the other thing, we look at those assessments and that literally drives what we do.... And that's what I want it to do. I don't want those just to come out as numbers.

Buffering Staff From Distractions to Their Work

A long line of research has reported the value of leaders protecting staff from being pulled in directions incompatible with agreed on goals. This buffering function reduces workload complexity by acknowledging the open nature of schools and the constant bombardment of staff with expectations from parents, the media, special interest groups, and the government (DiPaola & Tschannen-Moran, 2005). Internal buffering is also helpful, especially buffering teachers from excessive pupil disciplinary activity, a hedge against increased workload volume. One of our teacher interviewees described the buffering function as it was performed by her principal in these terms:

> She is very in tune to when we need a break from a kid, and she'll come grab the kid or let the kid know, you know if you're having a tough time or you can tell your students are having a tough time with you, just leave and come down to my office and sit and work for a while.

A principal described his buffering initiatives in these words:

> [I am] trying to make sure that teachers have the necessary tools in order to do the job well, that they really feel accountable for student learning,

> *that they maximize the time that they have with students ... by not interrupting their day. We minimize meetings ... so that they have time before school to plan. We try to be respectful of the time during the school day so they can plan with their colleagues and thus eliminate stress that some teachers have. Try not to overcommit them.*

The four sets of leadership practices associated with managing the instructional program act to ensure implementation and follow-through of those initiatives stimulated by the other leadership practices we have described. They also help provide the organizational stability necessary for improvement to occur.

CONCLUSION

At its core, successful leadership consists of pretty much the same set of practices wherever you find them; these practices, outlined in this and the previous chapter, are classified as Setting Directions, Developing People, Redesigning the Organization, and Managing the Instructional Program. Some of you will consider this an audacious claim. But here and elsewhere (e.g., Leithwood & Jantzi, 2005; Leithwood & Riehl, 2005), we have assembled a body of evidence in support of this claim that we think is quite compelling. The "audacity" of this claim is considerably softened, we expect, by our accompanying claim—that those leadership practices are successful only when they are enacted in ways that are highly sensitive to the contexts in which leaders find themselves. Our aim in these past two chapters has been to describe enactments of those successful leadership *basics* suitable to the *context* of teachers' emotional lives in school.

These chapters, however, have had nothing to say about how leaders might acquire whatever it takes to engage in these emotionally sensitive enactments. Does successful engagement depend on the emotional and social intelligence concepts popularized by Goleman (e.g., 1994, 2006)? He argued that such intelligences are learnable, and evidence about programs to further such learning, while modest in amount, is generally promising.

These are quite important issues to grapple with for those of us who argue that leading with teacher emotions in mind is a promising (albeit indirect) route to improving the learning of students. It is not an issue we address in much depth in this book. But we begin to nibble on it in the next and concluding chapter as a preview of things to come.

CHAPTER NINE

Conclusion

Leader Emotions

The previous two chapters have described what successful school leaders actually *do*. Based on a large body of evidence, these practices have been identified as effective for accomplishing a wide range of outcomes. For purposes of this book, however, it is their power to nurture positive teacher emotions that justifies our attention to this extended set of transformational leadership practices.

Knowing *what* successful school leaders actually do is obviously extraordinarily valuable for all kinds of reasons. Such awareness can inform leadership development initiatives and serve as a lens through which to view and assess a leader's performance. But knowing *what* successful leaders do begs questions about *how* and *why*. For instance, how do successful leaders sensitively adapt their practices to the emotional states of their teachers? What supports leaders in their efforts to build the dynamic learning communities so desperately needed in today's schools? How do they sustain themselves in the face of so many demands on their time, attention, and energy? Lacking well-informed answers to these questions compromises the effectiveness of leadership selection, development, and assessment efforts. We need to know more about what makes successful leaders tick. How do their internal states affect the way they run their schools? In particular, how do leaders develop the emotional preparedness they need to lead teachers successfully?

SOURCE: Material from Beatty, B. (2007, April). Inner leadership on the line. *Teacher, 182*(4) 12–17, is used with permission.

Those in formal leadership roles are de facto authority figures. They model how positional power is used and shape the culture in their organizations. If they are to provide supportive, encouraging leadership for learning among their colleagues, what support and encouragement for learning do leaders need? What are the key challenges affecting a leader's emotional states, and how do successful leaders handle the emotional issues in this complex work?

Until recently, educational leadership research has paid very little attention to these questions. Indeed, the democratic and egalitarian ethic currently driving much of the professional rhetoric about distributed and teacher leadership seems implicitly premised on the assumption that everyone can learn to lead, even without any specific preparation! Although we have no *philosophical* quarrel with such an ethic, and expect that everyone has known an excellent leader or two who may or may not have had formal training, the notion that leadership just emerges when one takes on this responsibility is a claim almost entirely lacking any empirical evidence. While most people are capable of becoming more skilled in most leadership functions, some develop these capacities much more readily than others and some to a much higher level. But if school leadership is to deliver on even a small portion of the great expectations now held for it, we can't settle for mediocrity. We need to become more sophisticated in identifying and developing people for performing at very high levels of leadership. The essence of the high-performing leader resides in core emotional preparedness to face the dangers, and dilemmas, with courage and a commitment to connectedness—to go in search of emotional common ground. This is a tall order indeed. Thus, we will explore some of the factors associated with an integrative approach to sustainable teaching, learning, leading, and living well in today's schools.

A great many factors in a leader's environment shape that person's actual practices, including, for example, educational policies, parental expectations, available resources, and the demands of supervisors. Leaders develop patterns in their practices in response to the on-the-job leadership opportunities that they happen to have experienced, the formal and informal mentoring they have received, and the professional development in which they have participated. But the actual effects of these external factors on leaders' overt practices are continuously mediated by their inner lives—their thoughts, feelings, values, and dispositions. These internal states act as interpretive fields for leaders, as they do for all people. In making sense of the world "out there," we are all affected by what we have become "in here." These are the silent sources of motivation for the practices leaders choose to enact. So what do we know about the inner lives of leaders and, in particular, their emotions?

We unpack the evidence about these emotions in two sections. The first section, adopting a "view from the outside looking in," relies primarily on evidence about the emotions of leaders working in nonschool contexts. This section assumes a broad conception of emotions, largely because of the nascent state of research in this area. The second section adopts "a view from the inside looking out" and is based on evidence collected exclusively from school leaders and teachers. Our discussion of this evidence is shaped, in substantial measure, by Beatty's research. It is a more "up close and personal" view of leader emotions at work and their consequences for both leaders and teachers.

A VIEW FROM THE OUTSIDE LOOKING IN

Much more evidence about leader emotions is available from research in nonschool than school organizations. As a sample of this evidence, we rely heavily on a particularly good review by Zaccaro, Kemp, and Bader (2004), which is informed primarily from data reported on between 1990 and 2003. The review was organized around a three-fold classification of leaders' affective states, including personality, motivation, and social appraisal skills. For purposes of this section, these three states are what we mean by *leader emotions.*

We compare the results of research reviewed by Zaccaro and his colleagues (2004) with the small amount of evidence available about these characteristics in school contexts. One source of such school-based evidence to which we consistently refer is a coordinated series of qualitative studies of successful principals in eight countries described in *Successful Principal Leadership: An International Perspective* edited by Day and Leithwood (2007).

Personality

In the case of personality, we extended the evidence reported by Zaccaro and his colleagues (2004) back in time by also drawing on a meta-analysis of empirical research reported between 1952 and 1991 (Barrick & Mount, 1991). Both of these reviews indicated that the vast majority of evidence about leaders' personalities has been conducted about what have been called for many years "the big five" leader personality factors. These include the following:

- *Emotional stability (anxious, depressed, angry, embarrassed, emotional, worried, insecure).* Maintaining emotional stability was significantly related to managerial effectiveness in Barrick and Mount's meta-analysis. The only school-based evidence we located about this trait came from the supportive results about the role of mood in expert leaders' problems. Leaders able to control their own moods—remain emotionally stable—engaged in more successful problem solving, all other things being equal.
- *Extraversion (sociable, gregarious, assertive, talkative, active).* Research on nonschool contexts, as captured in our two literature reviews, typically finds a significant association between extraversion and those holding formal leadership positions.
- *Agreeableness (courteous, flexible, trusting, good natured, cooperative, soft hearted, tolerant).* Barrick and Mount found no evidence that being agreeable had much to do with *managerial* success. Nonetheless, Zaccaro and his colleagues (2004), who focused on *leaders,* found significant relationships between successful leadership and a preference for social engagement (versus introspection). This preference for social engagement could well be interpreted as a link between extraversion and agreeableness.
- *Conscientiousness (hardworking, achievement oriented, persevering).* Both Zaccaro et al. and Barrick and Mount found relatively strong associations between this trait and leader success. Almost all of the five dozen principals included in the studies of successful leaders reported in Day and Leithwood (2007) demonstrated extreme versions of this trait. Even straightforward evidence about the typical length of current principals' workweeks (60–80 hours) makes an indirect but quite compelling case that hard work is a minimum requirement for survival (success aside) as a school administrator.

- *Openness to experience (imaginative, curious, original, broad-minded).* Barrick and Mount found openness associated most strongly with the likelihood that a leader would learn from educational experiences—be open to such learning. The successful principals described in Day and Leithwood (2007) were considered by teachers, parents, and students to be open and frank. The contribution of openness to leader success, while not unambiguous, was found to be generally positive in the review by Zaccaro et al. (2004); openness is often associated with a participatory leadership style (e.g., Blase & Anderson, 1995). Finally, the extent to which leaders are willing to share both school-related and personal information with their colleagues has been identified as a key factor in determining the extent to which teachers are willing to trust those in leadership positions (Tschannen-Moran & Hoy, 2000). Zaccaro and his colleagues concluded that

Taken together, these studies find robust associations between most of, if not all, the Big Five personality factors and leadership. Indeed Judge et al. (2002) report "a multiple correlation of .48 with leadership." (p. 112)

Additional evidence reviewed by Zaccaro et al. (2004) and reinforced by the evidence reported in Day and Leithwood (2007) links successful leadership to several personality traits beyond the "big five," notably optimism, proactivity (perhaps a correlate of extraversion), internal locus of control, and nurturance. But to date, relatively little in-depth research has been conducted into the inner workings of the links between most of these traits and successful *school* leadership.

With regard to transformational leadership, in particular, Popper and Mayseless (2002) summarized evidence indicating that these leaders have

a disposition for social dominance; a belief in the ability to influence others [self-efficacy beliefs]; a motivation and a capacity to treat others in a positive and encouraging way, while serving as role models; optimistic orientation toward the self, and others; and intellectual openness, curiosity and flexibility. (p. 215)

Leader self-efficacy (as with teacher self-efficacy) has been identified as an important antecedent to effective or transforming leadership in both the Zaccaro et al. (2004) and Popper and Mayseless (2002) reviews. Leadership research in school contexts has produced similar results (e.g., Leithwood & Jantzi, in press).

Motivation

Motivation is associated with the drive to satisfy needs. Zaccaro et al. (2004) claimed that the motives examined most in nonschool leadership contexts have been associated with the need for dominance or power, affiliation, achievement, and responsibility. Within our qualitative international project investigating successful school leaders, principals also demonstrated strong achievement needs (Gurr & Drysdale, 2007; Møller et al., 2007), but there was no evidence that successful school principals had a need for dominance, power, or affiliation. On the other hand, considerable evidence suggested that they were passionate about their work, highly committed emotionally, and highly motivated. Many of these school principals were perceived to have high energy levels likely to be motivational to others (Day, 2007; Gurr & Drysdale, 2007) as well as being determined, persistent, and industrious (e.g., Moos, Krejsler, Kofod, & Jensen, 2007). These motivational states of successful school principals seem to have no direct counterparts to the motives identified by Zaccaro et al. (2004), although a need for responsibility might be viewed as a distant relative of passion and commitment.

Social Appraisal Skills

The final category to be examined from the nonschool leadership research is social appraisal skills. Marlowe (1986) defined these skills as "the ability to understand the feelings, thoughts, and behaviors of persons, including oneself, in interpersonal situations and to act appropriately upon that understanding" (p. 52). Capacities included in this broad category refer to leaders' abilities to appreciate the emotional states of colleagues, to discern those states in complex social circumstances, to respond in ways that are considered helpful, and to understand and manage their own emotions. Zaccaro et al. (2004) linked variation in these skills with significant differences in leadership success.

Social and emotional "intelligence" are logically associated with social appraisal skills and have been the object of considerable noneducational leadership research, according to the Zaccaro et al. (2004) review. For instance, this research points to the importance of self-monitoring skills as well as other skills associated more particularly with emotional intelligence (EI). Conceptually, at the very least there is a clear resonance between Marlowe's notion of social appraisal skills and some facets of emotional intelligence. Mayer and Salovey described EI as

the ability to perceive accurately, appraise, and express emotion; the ability to access and/or generate feelings when they facilitate thought; the ability to understand emotion and emotional knowledge; and the ability to regulate emotions to promote emotional and intellectual growth. (p. 10)

In the international successful principals project (Day & Leithwood, 2007), five of the nine qualitative studies reported evidence of successful principals' being good listeners; one mentioned principals having a good sense of humor (Moos et al., 2007), which could be a sign of good social appraisal skills in some circumstances (e.g., a strategy for defusing conflict or reducing tension). Notably, the explicit evidence about successful principals reported by Day, Leithwood, and their colleagues does not reflect the full range of social appraisal skills uncovered in the wider leadership research. It is tempting, though, to infer from indirect evidence (such as the patterns among teachers' characterizations of successful school leaders) that quite extensive social appraisal skills are involved.

Associated with both EI and social appraisal skills is the "discernment" of what others are experiencing emotionally. This evokes the notion of empathy—used to sense "what people are feeling, being able to take their perspective, and cultivating rapport and attunement with a broad diversity of people" (Goleman, 1998, p. 318). While this certainly sounds positive and can be positive, dangers lurk beneath the surface of the leader who believes he knows what others are feeling. As Denzin (1984) argued, the belief that we can sense what others are feeling is just as often a mistaken belief; often, spurious emotionality is the result, as we can easily misinterpret another's feelings to be an extension of our own as we try to imagine what we might be feeling in their situation. Young (1997) argued that assuming we know another's feelings and preferences can be dangerous, especially if we are wrong. Only by engaging in respectful, reflective conversations to find out if what we have "sensed" is accurate can we hope to know what someone feels. Seeking deeper emotional understanding requires a willingness to enter the messy terrain of emotions *with others* (Denzin).

Boler (1999) cautioned that emotional intelligence is founded in a "universal portrait of human nature" (p. 74). This portrait ignores cultural diversity; "all gendered associations with emotion have been entirely erased"; and "the person" is conceived, somewhat like "the cognitive sciences of neurobiology and artificial intelligence," as emphasizing on "individualist survival" (p. 75). In contrast, we are discovering that school success relies on learning communities that celebrate interconnectedness and acknowledge interdependency. As global crises ranging from wealth to weather remind us, rugged individualism may deserve a rethink. The evolutionary power of emotion lies in the continual invention and reinvention, interpretation and reinterpretation of the self (Lupton, 1998) and the other (Margolis, 1998) in relationships.

Mastery of emotions in the service of an external authority does little to empower people for creative generative change from within. In education, the safety of a supportive school culture can act as a catalyst to transformation of a different kind, one that responds to real problems with genuine inquiry and authentic exploration of new possibilities. Fullan (2001) and others have signaled the importance of emotion to relationship building in educational leadership. Highly effective school leaders need to be much more than the smooth operators envisioned by Goleman (1998). Deeper levels of self-examination and emotional meaning making *with others* require school leaders to integrate their emotions not only in private processes but also in sense making *with* both their leader and teacher colleagues. Beyond emotional intelligence, this requires emotional wisdom and deep humility (Morris, Brotheridge, & Urbanski, 2005).

While empirical research that specifically explores the connections between the emotions of leadership and the measurable success of principals is in its infancy, the evidence about leadership in non-school settings that we have reviewed in this section indicates that, broadly speaking, social connectedness has a moderate to strong relationship with leadership success. This relationship seems to vary in strength depending on the type of job. Wong and Law suggested, for example, "that emotional management skills would be more strongly related to performance in highly emotionally laborious jobs than in those involving less emotional labor" (quoted in Zaccaro et al., 2004, p. 116). Emotional labor involves both masking and manufacturing emotions and is associated with significant side effects (Hochschild, 1983). School leadership undoubtedly qualifies as a "10" on the emotionally laborious scale.

A VIEW FROM THE INSIDE LOOKING OUT

This final section of the chapter and book ends with the beginning in mind. We have argued throughout that leaders can favorably impact students' learning conditions by attending to teachers' working conditions and their emotions. We have had glimpses of what teachers say about their leaders. What we have left to do, however, is to hear from the leaders themselves (principals will be the main focus in this section). This is not an oversight. You might say we have deliberately left the best for last. We mean this in the sense that leaders cannot be expected magically to manufacture emotional connectedness to teachers, or themselves for that matter, when the conditions of their work prevent this from happening. To change teachers' working conditions, leaders need to understand and address their own working conditions; that is, their inner working conditions. As we shall see, this is most likely to happen in connection with trusted others who are experiencing the same sorts of things, namely their principal peers.

Principals Talk About the Emotions of Leadership

It is true that in most of what we read and listen to, the emotional dimension does not get the focus it should. It doesn't seem to matter what I am dealing with—behaviour problems, students who excel and bring honour to the school, analysing public examination results, talking with parents, mediation, leading change . . . whatever, I am emotionally involved. (Australian principal)

We teach and lead from where we are as a human being. Therefore, it is essential to know who we are. (New Zealand principal)

As Gronn (1999) noted, leadership begins and ends with the self. The principals just quoted echo the importance of self-knowledge and point to connections among leader emotions, their selves, and their work (Beatty, 2002, 2005). Similarly, Caldwell (1997) maintained that in education, "success in the leadership of reform is as much a matter of discovering self as discovering strategy" (p. ix). Importantly, however, we need to appreciate the inseparability of emotions and self. Indeed,

> what is managed in an emotional experience is not an emotion but the self in the feeling that is being felt. . . . People are their emotions. To understand who a person is it is necessary to understand emotion." (Denzin, 1984, pp. 1, 50, 51)

First, we review some key findings from an intensive study of the emotions of leadership conducted with a group of 25 principals and headteachers[9] from six different countries—Canada, the United States, Australia, New Zealand, England, and Ireland—who joined each other over a seven-month period in a private, anonymous, asynchronous online discussion forum. The study aimed to provide a safe space for participants to discuss their own experiences (Beatty, 2002, 2005) and continued the work of breaking the silence (Beatty, 2000a) on the emotional realities of school leadership. The project ended up winning a Canadian national award, suggesting perhaps that the time was right for emotions to begin to take their rightful place in educational leadership research, theory, and practice. We also refer to studies involving 50 Ontario teachers in interviews about their recalled emotionally positive and negative experiences with school administrators and recollections from students of emotional leadership in Masters courses in the United States and Australia (Beatty, 2002, 2006, 2007a; Beatty & Brew, 2004).

Early in their online discussions, the principals and headteachers were surprised to discover that whether they were in small or large, rural or urban, primary or secondary, private or public settings, emotionally speaking, they all seemed to be doing the same job:

---

9. In England and Ireland, principals are referred to as headteachers.

> *I am surprised at how much of the emotional experiences outlined are similar to those I know. (Canadian principal)*
>
> *I can identify with much of what I read here. (Irish headteacher)*
>
> *It seems like we are all in the same building, experiencing the same sorts of things. (Canadian principal)*
>
> *Across the world, we all have the same kinds of difficulties and problems—some to different degrees. I like to see that the same things make us tick as well. Is that what keeps us going as leaders? (Irish headteacher)*

The online leaders immediately agreed that their jobs often involved a chaotic whirl of unpredictability and quickly recognized that, where emotions were concerned, their first job was to control and even hide them altogether:

> *At one point today, I was in my office with several staff members, participating in a School Based Team meeting to address the learning needs of some of Grade 1 students experiencing difficulties, when an emergency call from FACS (Family and Children Services) came in. At the same time, our Student Services Consultant arrived and wanted to meet. Add the call from the parent wanting to express her bus concerns. Through all this, one attempts to maintain composure, sift through the information to identify the immediate needs, and basically juggle the rest. At all times, maintaining composure and not saying what you would like to say. (Canadian principal)*

Further exemplifying the highly-managed emotional self, a Canadian principal believed he had his verbal expression of emotion under control but was continuing to work on being careful not to even raise an eyebrow:

> *I have caught myself in an emotional turmoil on occasion. Not so much displaying verbal discontentment, but utilizing body language that would indicate that I was not impressed with the situation. I am trying to alter that reaction as I feel that I need to remain calm & poised in all situations. I'm still pondering this & no doubt I'll come back to it in the future. (Canadian principal)*

Across the seven-month online conversation, several themes emerged, while emotional labor and its attendant drain remained a common thread throughout. First up was the toll of government policy pressures. Again we see the intensification associated with the imperative to remain highly emotionally managed at all times:

Our department has just offered us a new award, which removes 4 weeks of principals' holidays for not much money. We are all feeling under-valued, morale is low and there is significant industrial action taking place. I am about to leave for an induction of new Year 7 parents so will attempt to regroup mentally and convey positive and exciting messages. (Australian principal)

In their role as policy mediators, principals have a lot to manage:

As principal I feel I am somewhat of the gatekeeper, I have the responsi-bility to implement policy, however, I also have the power to manage and ensure that we don't totally drown in the policy shift. (Canadian principal)

But when policies shift back and forth, these leaders were regularly dusted with the emotional fallout:

A new government has now been elected ... and they are carrying through their election promise of abolishing bulk funding. ... It means I will employ fewer teachers next year, class sizes will increase, noncontact periods will decrease, and worst of all, a highly successful program ... for our less able students will have to go. ... How do I feel? So frustrated, disheartened, and very, very angry. ... I could scream. (New Zealand principal)

Changing policies often place principals "in the middle," with pressures to continue to feature the moral purpose of doing what's best for kids, while honoring their professional obligation to the governing body that is changing the policy. This regularly places them at odds with parents, teachers, and their own consciences:

> *When the LEA [Local Educational Authority] changes its policy to do with Special Needs... leaving me to face parents whose expectations are dashed and leave them nowhere to turn, they focus their anger and frustration on me. I feel as if I have won the lottery but can't have any of the money. This feeling of powerlessness was most acute in my early years as a Headteacher. In the first term, I often wondered why I had taken up the post.... Having the responsibility without ultimate power can be deadening. (U.K. headteacher)*

This "deadening" effect is reminiscent of Hochschild's (1983) finding that perpetual emotional labor causes emotional numbness. Such numbness threatens well-being and compromises the ability to connect emotionally with self and others. In the case above, the leader's self is divided—having to *manufacture* the emotional strength to embrace her mandated responsibility and *mask* her own very real frustrations and actual disapproval of the policy as well as *manage* the anger of the parents.

The link between emotional labor and emotional numbness is critical to our considerations of school leaders and teachers. Emotional numbness goes some of the way toward explaining their traditional disconnection from each other. Teachers and principals regularly operate from the belief that the other just doesn't understand or appreciate what they are going through (Beatty, 2002). But let us delve deeper into the role that the professional culture plays in maintaining emotional silence and thereby the working conditions that foster emotional distance and disconnection from one another.

With each new education policy initiative, there is a "moral push" for teachers and leaders to suffer in silence and simply comply with the demand to implement, whether they agree or not. This is part of what Connelly and Clandinin (1995) called the "sacred story":

In policy deliberation... there is no entry point for debate and discussion of the funneled materials. They, necessarily, must be taken as givens. To debate their appropriateness is to question someone's authority. Discussion, such as it is, is removed from matters of substance to matters of personality and power.... Everything comes with a moral push with which teachers [and leaders] are expected to do something. This moral orientation and sense of persuasion are due to the sacred story, which required that the "descriptive 'is' of theoretical knowledge be transformed into a prescriptive 'ought' in practice." The conduit is prescriptive; it is a conduit of shoulds. (p. 11)

Managing the constant demands emanating from this conduit of shoulds and making sure one is seen to be compliant are what Ball (2000) referred to as the pressures of performativity. This is part of the emotional labor inherent in the work of both teachers and leaders. Particularly poignant—emotionally and relationally speaking—is the fact that when leaders manufacture their enthusiasm to appear to endorse each new policy, they also position themselves as the authority that embodies the policy. This effectively silences debate and precludes the candor that could bring teachers and leaders together in a shared understanding of their emotional and professional common ground. Instead, the gulf typically widens. Leaders and teachers regularly find themselves wounded and wounding as the flack from these unresolved tensions begins to fly.

While online, our study's leaders were reclaiming their right to their actual emotions. In the safety of their privacy with each other, they regularly wrote of the imperative to control and mask their real feelings and generate the impression of feeling differently than they did. To achieve convincingly these acts of emotional display and masking, one option is to wall off actual feelings within one's self. This desensitizes and thereby disconnects people from others as they go into a kind of emotionally disengaged autopilot, as it were. The issue with ongoing emotional labor (EL) (and teachers are no strangers to EL) is that it creates a divided self, one that is literally disintegrated. This phenomenon, over time, causes people actually to become emotionally numb—numb to the inner signals from one's emotions and to the signals from others and their obvious and hidden emotion states. The condition that results is actually very dangerous, as it separates us from the very survival system we have relied upon over the ages, creating emotional imbalance and even mental illness (Greenberg & Paivio, 1997); it ensures continued social detachment and all of its associated implications.

The compounded side effects from prolonged emotional labor are serious, systemic, and inherent in the notion of defining *professional* as "unemotional." This stance is regularly played out in the espousal of pseudo-objectivity in leaders' and teachers' dealings with each other. Emotions are always present, whether we acknowledge them or not (Damasio, 1997). The point is that, while emotional labor is required and inherent in the work of both teachers and leaders and retention of emotional control is essential and desirable, the denial of inner emotional realities to lessen the strain of emotional labor is neither innocuous nor benign. Emotions are the fabric of the self, and our awareness and responsiveness to them serves to keep us socially linked, individually centered, and in touch with our personal and professional ethics (Margolis, 1998). From a state of emotional numbness, these things are much harder to accomplish.

Without the opportunity to address and reintegrate these emotional tensions—consciously and explicitly—what suffers is leaders' and teachers' well-being and their ability to stay connected with their inner selves and each other. This is where the importance of reflecting with trusted colleagues comes in. In the online forum, the international group of school leaders shared stories of both helpful and threatening parents, endangered and damaging students, and some of the long-term effects that both emotional and physical woundings had inflicted upon them. They found their online conversations an exotic departure from anything they had experienced before. Together, they were reclaiming their whole selves and found the process was meeting a need:

> At the beginning, I found it difficult to find time; now it's a "treat" to get online. The conversations have made me reflect so much more, consider my approaches, applaud my colleagues online, wherever they are. . . . I've mentioned this forum, although not its contents, and the majority response has been "how do you find the time?" Now I know I need to find the time. (U.K. headteacher)

> It is about feeling known. I can't help feeling that this virtual world is more powerful than the real version. Of course what people say and the responses they make to me in the real world are important. . . . but this all has an extra "frisson" about it. (another U.K. headteacher)

As they connected with each other, they began to experiment with the opportunities to play with ideas that the online forum was providing. One participant suggested they exchange images of themselves, resulting in self-characterizations such as the tireless "energizer bunny," androgynous "Captain Kirk and the good mother," invisibly adaptive "chameleon," Web conscious "female (not black widow) spider," and "benevolent coordinator/despot—still benevolent Fat Controller (from Thomas the Tank Engine)." These images provided richly evocative glimpses about the ways these leaders were seeing themselves in action. Issues of gender bias, lack of time, emotional and social isolation, impacts on their own families, and the value of their leadership teammates all helped to provide color and texture to the tapestry of inner leadership life that they were weaving together. These themes are discussed in more depth elsewhere (Beatty, 2002, 2005, 2006).

I Am My School

A principal's emotional connection to the job and a particular school can be a tremendous asset. However, there is also emotional risk when a principal becomes so strongly identified with the school (Loader, 1997; Southworth, 1998) that she finds it hard to separate what people say about the schools from what they are saying about the principal. A U.K. headteacher had been living with the constant concern that "the great Ofsted [Office for Standards in Education, Children's Services and Skills] will come in and label us a failing school!" She felt "drained" and "frustrated" when progress was slow. Presumably, such a label would also imply that she was a failing principal. As Loader noted,

> Criticisms of my school were taken personally, as criticisms of me. With this mind set it became very hard to have a private life. . . . My personal failure was that I had no sense of myself as separate from the institution. (p. 147)

There were definite signs of workaholism (Killinger, 1991) in these online principals' profiles. Perhaps in identifying so strongly with their role as champions of the whole school, leaders may be more easily understood in terms of their high expectations of themselves and others. In any case, it was clear that these leaders were powerfully motivated by the satisfactions and joys of the work and were experiencing a clear passion of purpose:

I would have died for that school! . . . I truly enjoy my work. I cannot think of any other job I'd rather do. I cannot think of any other place I would have the opportunity to be so many things to so many people. There is great joy and pleasure in seeing a child succeed. Yet there is no greater pleasure than seeing a teacher succeed. (U.K. headteacher)

What Is It About the Teacher-Leader Relationship?

Given the shared demands on teachers and formal leaders, one might expect them to stick together. Yet in the field, and acknowledged in the literature for some time, the teacher-leader relationship remains problematic (Huberman 1993; Lortie, 1975; Starratt, 1991). While increasingly expected to collaborate and even share leadership responsibilities, teachers and principals have a hard time getting and staying connected to one another. While they converge over career, colleagues, parents, students, and organizational procedures, they have sometimes complementary but often conflicting concerns. Administrative leaders' interactions with teachers create emotional dynamics that position leaders variously as evaluators, mutually caring colleagues, and, sometimes, professional supporters. Their styles and qualities of communication and emotional attunement shape and reflect their level of engagement with teachers (Beatty, 2002, 2007a). In Beatty's study, emerging consistently both from teachers' positive and negative recollections of administrators, was their stated desire for more contact and interconnectedness with their leaders. So why is this so hard to accomplish for so many leaders and teachers? What about the leader-teacher relationship might leaders' emotional experiences help us understand? Let us turn to the leaders themselves for some insights.

Online, the leaders became increasingly aware of the desirability of connecting emotionally with teachers and began seeing it as part of their job. But they were finding it difficult to imagine how to accomplish this in the midst of the usual fray:

How I communicate with others in my work situation requires a "sense of the other." This isn't always easy when I'm racing at a million miles an hour to solve on the spot problems. To be able to pick up the emotional signs of those with whom I work should enable me to better help them in their daily tasks and therefore help me to do my job. (Australian principal)

These leaders noted that their usual role was more of being an emotional cheerleader, which didn't leave much room for delving into difficulties:

> I am particularly conscious of the need and importance of setting a positive, cheerful and understanding tone each day to counteract the negatives that some staff members carry with them into the building. (Canadian principal)

These principals were beginning to recognize the need to connect emotionally with their teachers. At the same time, they were inclined to project onto teachers an expectation that principals must seem strong. This left them emotionally masked and unable to make a genuine person-to-person connection:

> One of the fears of leadership is exposing too many weaknesses. Not many staff feel more confident after learning that their principal is struggling to cope day by day. . . . Why do I mask my emotions? Usually when the conversation I am in is an emotional issue for the other person, emotionally challenging I mean. There are lots of things that I can and do share, like elation, grief, etc. but the times when I try to be calm and very rational are when there is an issue that is bringing out the worst in a teacher or parent. Responding angrily to anger is like throwing petrol on a fire. (New Zealand principal)

Arguably, such emotional separation, while seen as required, may at the same time be compromising leaders' sense of the other by numbing their emotional self (Hochschild, 1983). This concern had not escaped this same New Zealand principal, as she revisited the issue later:

> When I'm doing something I find hard to do, I used to become quite matter-of-fact and I thought, businesslike. It was seen as being cold. The conversations about someone's competence are not aided by being delivered in a way that adds to the problem—or creates a new one. I have had to learn how to have the difficult conversations, which I hate, without losing my rapport with the person. The relationship still has to function without me withdrawing because I feel awful, or awkward. . . . I am warm and emotional at home but find it difficult to be so at school with teachers.

So where is the place for emotional honesty and shared emotional meaning making in these teacher-leader interactions? While connecting emotionally may have transformational potential, it is not without its challenges or perils. Otherwise, it would be common practice. And it is not.

Preparing to Address the Emotions in Teacher-Leader Relationships

What if, in contrast to the typically emotionally laundered professional discourse among educators, leaders were to lead themselves and others from an emotional perspective and practice emotional meaning making in reflection, alone and with others? Could they lead the reculturing of their schools so that everyone could come to use emotionally grounded approaches to solving problems in living and learning together? By positioning the solvency of relationships as foundational to everything else, findings from the online forum leader study indicate that participants found themselves and their professional practice to be transformed by the experience:

> *I was moved by some of the comments made, it caused me to think about me and the way I respond to people and situations. It will be some time before my immediate response is to beat up myself. I have had to stop and take time out to think about the me that seems to be disappearing under the initiatives and reforms from the "faceless ones," underperforming teachers and aggressive and abusive parents and children. I think I am more reflective.*

> *I was privileged to be part of just seeing and knowing how much we all react to the emotional dimension about our jobs and our lives . . . so often we don't see that when we are talking in groups/at meetings etc. I guess in those situations we tend to want to show that we are on top of all the situations thrown at us and we don't let people see how we really feel.*

> *The "emotions of leadership" has [sic] played an important part in my consciousness. . . . Just knowing how angry, upset, happy etc. other people get has allowed me to feel OK about the way I feel. I guess the privilege of being part of the conversations has been to legitimize MY feelings, and to go with them, rather than try to block them out. . . . We work with people and their emotions and their "emotional baggage" all day every*

> *day. Being able to talk on line about feelings was not only cathartic, it has helped me acknowledge the emotions of my staff members more openly.*
>
> *In answer to your question about the leadership conversations, and whether they had any effects on my leadership, I think the answer is still yes, even such a time after I was able to take a regular part. . . . I learned through other people's contributions that a recognition of your own and other people's emotions is a positive force for good, but I also learnt to see that it means you have to handle the negative emotions, too, and analyse and respond to them as well.*

Studies of leader preparation programs that deliberately and explicitly integrate experiential learning about emotions and leadership are beginning to suggest that school leaders may indeed be able to reculture their schools to become safe places for genuine inquiry.

Approaches to leadership development that are designed to help principals become emotionally prepared for addressing challenging situations in emotionally attuned and interpersonally supportive ways have been implemented in the United States and Australia, with emerging signs of success (see Beatty, 2006, 2007a; Beatty & Brew, 2004). In a U.S. setting, leadership students were beginning to connect their own experiences with the theories of emotional leadership. Said one student:

> *To develop the constructive teacher administrator relationship, the administrator must be willing to show the teacher that he or she cares. In my situation, my principal can show me that she cares by building a significant relationship with me. She can make an attempt to know my personality, interests, and strengths. She also lets me know about her, and what makes her "tick." When she is personally vulnerable, she shows me that she trusts me.*

Other applications include the custom-designed Master in School Leadership (MSL) at Monash University in Melbourne, Australia. By positioning emotions as foundational and using an experiential and developmental approach, the course moves leaders in their practice from emotional silence to emotional reflection and collaboration, from emotional absolutism that dictates what is "right" and "wrong" to feel, and an adherence to dysfunctional feeling rules to a more expansive transitional stance within which emotional relativism and the scope of professional relationships can be discovered and explored (Beatty, 2002, 2005, 2007b). Emotional knowledge authority is reclaimed and becomes increasingly internal. The result is an emotional resilience and nonanxious presence (Friedman, 1985) for working creatively and constructively with others.

By making emotions explicit, leadership preparation courses, such as the Monash model, can catalyze inner change. But this is a definite departure from the posture of leadership as grooming oneself for donning borrowed robes. In a study of the impact on students of the Monash MSL course, a recent graduate commented

> *You can give lip service to emotions, but until you're forced into reflecting and working with people in that way, you don't actually change. And I think that's what's happened for me over the last two years is that [with emphasis and deep conviction] I've changed!*

The leaders in this Monash MSL course are encouraged to identify and face their fears, revisit inevitable experiences of having been wounded, and learn to value and protect their entitlement to their own humanness and imperfection. This new breed of leader is becoming emotionally prepared to transcend the need to direct and confront and is learning to reframe conflict as an opportunity to build relationships. The same recent Monash MSL graduate said

> *Underneath I saw myself—I knew that it was wrong—and yet other people expected me to be fully formed as a leader, . . . I felt like a phoney. Someone's going to find out that I don't know everything. I'm going to make mistakes, and I shouldn't be making mistakes at this stage in my career! . . . So in terms of now, I see myself as—I'm a work in progress. . . .*
>
> *What I've noticed with emotions is that if you do that in a confrontational way, what you get is resistance, anger and frustration. If you invite someone and work along side then you get excitement, engagement and change. . . . Instead of the expert, I was learning too. . . . Before I would have run away from people feeling upset. I would have thought that they needed to recover themselves, and . . . not mention it again rather than tackle it as a way of building trust.*

Emotional leadership is relational leadership, and it begins with the emotions of leaders themselves. Another graduate, who had taken on a new principalship, was grateful for having learned how to practice emotional meaning making:

> I'm not a very empathetic person by nature and definitely not very emotional. And I've sort of had to confront that within my self as well. . . . [In a situation with warring parents on the school council], I'd actually acknowledged that these emotions that were floating around between the two groups were affecting me as well. So I think that worked really well. And if I hadn't done that, the shooting from the hip, the nasty comments, the snide remarks would have escalated. And it just made people more aware that they were actually talking about people who were working for the same thing.
>
> It's very hard to be a good technical leader without having strong relationships with people you're working with. A good technical leader without the relationships would be more likely the efficient tyrant, rather than someone who is able to get the best out of their people—because people want to do their best. . . . The whole feel of the school is based on relationships. I can't imagine where I'd be in five years from now without the whole development of relationships through emotions.

Some validation of the power of emotions is needed so that teachers and leaders can observe together how their feelings are affecting their interpretations of situations and each other. Conversely, retaining a "professional" silence about emotions serves only to increase their intensity and undermine the pursuit of collaborative professional potential. Building community and fostering relationships go hand in hand. Emotions cannot be banished like pesky interlopers (Beatty, 2000a) if leaders and teachers are to get to the bottom of their issues with each other and strengthen their relationships in the process.

Leaders often conclude that it is better not to feel anything at all, or at least to seem not to be having emotions, for fear of being revealed and thereby disempowered. The distinction between (1) feeling a feeling, considering consciously one's own feelings and those of others, and (2) displaying feelings in the moment is an important one. The fear and shame of feeling at all gets tangled up with the erroneous assumption that by letting oneself feel and by reflecting about one's own and others' feelings, all hell will break loose. The anticipation of shame and humiliation is a powerful disincentive to consider emotions at all. The fear of loss of power is inherent in leadership. Yet a reign of rule-by-fear begets leaders who are frightened, too. Addressing the absurdity of this reinforcing spiral may be counterintuitive for leaders, who are often inducted by models of outmoded "my-way-or-the-highway" styles. The fully integrated, multidimensional self can afford to be genuine and curious, even uncertain at times, which can create openings for consultation and collaboration. As one participant in the MSL graduate study said,

> I've—finally, finally, finally—moved into my own as a leader. I've found my own place in terms of how to deal with things. And I've found a place that I'm satisfied with. I've found a place that is a fit for me and is reflective of me. It's not reflective of my mentor and who he is. It's not my previous assistant principal. It's not reflective of anyone. It's who I am! There's a lot of personal pride and joy in that. I'm quite proud of myself, that I actually had the guts.

When leaders neglect to consider their own and others' emotions and are not supported in discovering how emotional meaning-making systems are relevant to relationships, they regularly objectify others as troublemakers, or blockers, in the attempt to assume away their problematic nature by categorizing them. In the reductionism of negating or ignoring the emotional dimension of the problematic persons, only the fallout on others gets attention, and the person whose issues were the original provocation becomes typecast as a villain and neglected.

The notion that one must suspend a relationship with a colleague to deal with professional issues (suggested early in the online discussion forum by one of the participants) is an example of the *paradox of emotion and educational leadership:* the dichotomy between the way leaders and teachers believe they must seem and the ways (as highly functioning, fully dimensional people) they need to be. By counterintuitively moving toward the "danger" (Maurer, 1996) and leaning into their fears, leaders can learn to embrace a pedagogy of discomfort (Boler, 1999) and discover the rightful place of their integrated selves in their work. When they do so, they are emotionally prepared to connect with their teachers and address the emotional implications of teachers working conditions and, correspondingly, students' learning conditions.

CONCLUSION

If leaders want teachers to respond creatively and constructively to the pressures for collaborative improvement in their practices, they need to model the courage it takes to face the emotional discomfort associated with such an imperative. To invite emotional candor, they need to offer it first, conveying their own sense of vulnerability as a basis for mutual understanding. Making emotional meaning together is a powerful and transformational endeavor. Gaining emotional knowledge is engendered by dynamic emotional engagement on both sides, which fosters the ethic of mutuality, shared humanness, and the discovery of the emotional common ground we envisioned in the opening paragraphs of this chapter. The notion of the leader as merely thinking about others' feelings, rather than *feeling with others,* is a critical distinction. Beyond emotional cleverness, or even emotional intelligence, whereby leaders read others' emotions and anticipate their feelings in order to influence them, we invite leaders to embrace with courage and conviction the challenges of creating new emotional knowledge and understanding *together with* teachers. A world of possibilities awaits schools whose leaders develop such cultures of care and connectedness.

> I believe that creating an environment where teachers feel free to expand, take risks, initiate projects is so important. The full issue of trust is front and centre. Knowing that they are valued, able to initiate the project or activity (always discussed prior to) inviting feedback is a powerful way to encourage teachers to grow. I have several staff members who are those risk takers, doing what is good for kids and going that extra mile. Taking those risks can sometimes be an uncomfortable yet an exciting place. They know that the door is always open for the discussion, to guide to reinforce to redirect to support. This is the same group that motivates or pushes along the others. Perhaps some would see it as a giving up of power. I would prefer to view it as shared administration. Our goal is to do what benefits the children. . . . Motivated teachers is that. (Canadian principal)

Teachers and leaders who let themselves be known by inviting each other into their emotional worlds can provide each with a greater sense of the other to great effect for the working conditions of both teachers and leaders and the benefit of society's children.[10]

10. A wide range of resources for leaders to commence their inner journeys can be accessed by pursuing further study, such as the Monash Master in School Leadership, and/or participating in face-to-face study and support groups or online discussion forums for principals. Readers are welcome to contact Dr. Brenda Beatty for more information on any or all of these opportunities: brenda.beatty@education.monash.edu.au.

References

Anderman, E., & Wolters, C. (2006). Goals, values, and affect: Influences on student motivation. In P. Alexander & P. Winne (Eds.), *Handbook of educational psychology* (2nd ed., pp. 369–390). London: Erlbaum.

Anderson, R., Greene, M., & Loewen, P. (1988). Relationships among teachers' and students' thinking skills, sense of efficacy, and student achievement. *Journal of Educational Research, 34*(2), 148–165.

Angle, H. L., & Perry, J. L. (1981). An empirical assessment of organizational commitment and organizational effectiveness. *Administrative Science Quarterly, 26*(1), 1–14.

Armor, D., Conroy-Oseguera, P., Cox, M., King, N., McDonnell, L., Pascall, A., et al. (1976). *Analysis of the school preferred reading programs in Los Angeles minority schools* (Report No. R-2007-LAUSD). Santa Monica, CA: Rand Corporation (abstract available from ERIC Document Reproduction Service No. ED130243).

Ashton, P. T., & Webb, R. B. (1986). *Making a difference: Teachers' sense of efficacy and student achievement.* New York: Longman Group United Kingdom.

Avolio, B. J. (1994). The alliance of total quality and the full range of leadership. In B. M. Bass & B. J. Avolio (Eds.), *Improving organizational effectiveness through transformational leadership* (pp. 121–145). Thousand Oaks, CA: SAGE.

Avolio, B. J., & Gardner, W. (2005). Authentic leadership development: Getting to the root of positive forms of leadership. *The Leadership Quarterly, 16*(3), 315–338.

Ball, S. (2000). Performativities and fabrications in the education economy: Towards the performative society. *Australian Educational Researcher, 27*(2), 1–25.

Bandura, A. (1977). Self-efficacy: Toward a unifying theory of behavioral change. *Psychological Review, 84*(2), 191–215.

Bandura, A. (1982). Self-efficacy and mechanism in human agency. *American Psychologist, 37*(2), 122–147.

Bandura, A. (1986). *Social foundations of thought and action.* Englewood Cliffs, NJ: Prentice Hall.

Bandura, A. (1990). Self-regulation of motivation through anticipatory and self-regulatory mechanisms. In R. A. Dienstbier (Ed.), *Perspectives on motivation: Nebraska symposium on motivation* (Vol. 38, pp. 69–164). Lincoln: University of Nebraska Press.

Bandura, A. (1993). Perceived self-efficacy in cognitive development and functioning. *Educational Psychologist, 28*(2), 117–148.

Bandura, A. (1996). *Self-efficacy in changing societies.* New York: Cambridge University Press.

Bandura, A. (1997). *Self-efficacy: The exercise of control.* New York: W. H. Freeman and Company.

Banki, S. (2006). *Effect of transformational leadership on organization citizenship behaviour of teachers.* Toronto, ON: University of Toronto.

Bar-On, R. (1988). *The development of a concept of psychological well-being.* Unpublished doctoral dissertation, Rhodes University, South Africa.

Barrick, M. R., & Mount, M. K. (1991). The big five personality dimensions and job performance: A meta-analysis. *Personnel Psychology, 44*(1), 1–26.

Bass, B. M. (1985). *Leadership and performance beyond expectations.* New York: Free Press.

Bass, B. M., & Avolio, B. J. (1994). *Improving organizational effectiveness through transformational leadership.* Thousand Oaks, CA: SAGE.

Bateman, J., & Organ, D. (1983). Job satisfaction and the good soldier: The relationship between affect and employee "citizenship." *Academy of Management Journal, 26*(4), 587–595.

Bateman, J., & Strasser, S. (1984). A longitudinal analysis of the antecedents of organizational commitment. *Academy of Management Journal, 27*(1), 95–112.

Baylor, A., & Ritchie, D. (2002). What factors facilitate teacher skill, teacher morale, and perceived student learning in technology-using classrooms? *Computers and Education, 39*(4), 395–414.

Beatty, B. (2000a). The emotions of educational leadership: Breaking the silence. *International Journal of Leadership in Education, 3*(4), 331–358.

Beatty, B. (2000b). Teachers leading their own professional growth: Self-directed reflection and collaboration and changes in perception of self and work in secondary school teachers. *International Journal of In-Service Education, 26*(1), 73–97.

Beatty, B. (2002). *Emotion matters in educational leadership: Examining the unexamined.* Unpublished doctoral dissertation, Ontario Institute for Studies in Education, University of Toronto, Toronto, ON.

Beatty, B. (2005). Emotional leadership. In B. Davies (Ed.), *The essentials of school leadership.* Thousand Oaks, CA: Corwin Press.

Beatty, B. (2006). Becoming emotionally prepared for leadership: Courage, counter-intuition, and commitment to connectedness. *International Journal of Knowledge, Culture and Change Management, 6*(5), 51–66.

Beatty, B. (2007a). Feeling the future: Learning to lead with the emotions in mind. *Leading and Managing, 13*(2), 44–65.

Beatty, B. (2007b). Going Through the Emotions: Leadership that gets to the heart of school renewal. *Australian Journal of Education, 51*(3), 328–340.

Beatty, B., & Brew, C. (2004). Trusting relationships and emotional epistemologies: A foundational leadership issue. *School Leadership and Management, 24*(3), 329–356.

Belliveau, G., Liu, X., & Murphy, E. (2002). *Teacher workload on Prince Edward Island.* Charlottetown, PEI: Prince Edward Island Teachers' Federation.

Bempah, E. O., Kaylen, M. S., Osburn, D. D., & Birkenholz, R. J. (1994). An econometric analysis of teacher mobility. *Economics of Education Review, 13*(1), 69–77.

Bennis, W., & Nanus, B. (1985). *Leaders: The strategies for taking charge.* New York: Harper & Row.

Black, S. (2001). Morale matters: When teachers feel good about their work, research shows, student achievement rises. *American School Board Journal, 188*(1), 40–43.

Blase, J., & Anderson, G. (1995). *The micropolitics of educational leadership: From control to empowerment.* London: Cassell Education.

Blase, J., & Blase, J. (2001). *Empowering teachers: What successful principals do* (2nd ed.). Thousand Oaks, CA: Corwin Press.

Blase, J. J., & Greenfield, W. (1985). How teachers cope with stress: How administrators can help. *The Canadian Administrator, 25*(2), 1–5.

Boies, K., & Howell, J. M. (2006). Leader-member exchange in teams: An examination of the interaction between relationship differentiation and mean LMX in explaining team-level outcomes. *Leadership Quarterly, 17*(3), 246–257.

Boler, M. (1999). *Feeling power: Emotions and education.* New York: Routledge.

Briggs, L. D., & Richardson, W. D. (1992). Causes and effects of low morale among secondary teachers. *Journal of Instructional Psychology, 19*(2), 87–92.

Brouwers, A., & Tomic, W. (2000). A longitudinal study of teacher burnout and perceived self-efficacy in classroom management. *Teaching and Teacher Education, 16*(2), 239–253.

Buchanan, B. (1974). Building organizational commitment: The socialization of managers in work organization. *Administrative Science Quarterly, 19*(4), 533–546.

Buckley, J., Schneider, M., & Shang, Y. (2005). Fix it and they might stay: School facility quality and teacher retention in Washington, D.C. *Teachers College Record, 107*(5), 1107–1123.

Burns, J. M. (1978). *Leadership.* New York: Harper & Row.

Byrne, B. M. (1991). Burnout: Investigating the impact of background variables for elementary, intermediate, secondary, and university educators. *Teaching and Teacher Education, 7*(2), 197–209.

Caldwell, B. (1997). Prologue: The external principal. In D. Loader (Ed.), *The inner principal* (pp. vii–ix). London: Falmer.

Chan, D. W. (2002). Stress, self-efficacy, social support, and psychological distress among prospective Chinese teachers in Hong Kong. *Educational Psychology, 22*(5), 557–569.

Connelly, F. M., & Clandinin, D. J. (1995). Teachers' professional knowledge: Secret, sacred and cover stories. In F. M. Connelly & D. J. Clandinin (Eds.), *Teachers' professional knowledge landscapes* (pp. 1–15). New York: Teachers College Press.

Crow, G., & Pounder, D. G. (1997, March). *Faculty teams: Work group enhancement as a teacher involvement strategy.* Paper presented at the annual meeting of the American Educational Research Association, Chicago, IL.

Csikzentmihalyi, M. (1990). *The psychology of optimal experience.* New York: Harper & Row.

Cunningham, W. J. (1983). Teacher burnout—solutions for the 1980s: A review of the literature. *The Urban Review, 15*(1), 37–49.

Currivan, D. (2000). The causal order of job satisfaction and organizational commitment in models of employee turnover. *Human Resources Management Review, 9*(4), 495–524.

Damasio, A. (1997). *Descartes' error: Emotion, reason, and the human brain* (2nd ed.). New York: Avon.

Dannetta, V. (2002). What factors influence a teacher's commitment to student learning? *Leadership and Policy in Schools, 1*(2), 144–171.

Datnow, A., & Castellano, M. (2000). Teachers' responses to success for all: How beliefs, experiences, and adaptations shape implementation. *American Educational Research Journal, 24*(2), 775–799.

Day, C. (2007). Sustaining success in challenging contexts: Leadership in English schools. In C. Day & K. Leithwood (Eds.), *Successful principal leadership: An international perspective.* Dordrecht, The Netherlands: Springer.

Day, C., Hadfield, M., & Harris, A. (1999, September). *Leading schools in times of change.* Paper presented at the European Conference on Educational Research, Lahti, Finland.

Day, C., Harris, A., Hadfield, M., Tolley, H., & Beresford, J. (Eds.). (2000). *Leading schools in times of change.* Buckingham, UK: Open University Press.

Day, C., & Leithwood, K. (Eds.). (2007). *Successful principal leadership in times of change: An international perspective.* Dordrecht, The Netherlands: Springer..

Day, C., Stobart, G., Sammons, P., Kington, A., Gu, Q., Smees, R., et al. (2006). Variations in teachers' work, lives and effectiveness (Reference No. RR743). London: Department for Education and Skills.

De Maeyer, S., Rymenans, R., Van Petegem, P., van der Bergh, H., & Rijlaarsdam, G. (2006). *Educational leadership and pupil achievement: The choice of a valid conceptual model to test effects in school effectiveness research.* Unpublished manuscript: University of Antwerp, Belgium.

Denzin, N. K. (1984). *On understanding emotion.* San Francisco: Jossey-Bass.

Dibbon, D. (2004). *It's about time: A report on the impact of workload on teachers and students.* Memorial University of Newfoundland, St. John's, NL.

Dinham, S., & Scott, C. (1998). A three domain model of teacher and school executive satisfaction. *Journal of Educational Administration, 36*(4), 362–378.

Dinham, S., & Scott, C. (2000). Moving into the third, outer domain of teacher satisfaction. *Journal of Educational Administration, 38*(4), 379–396.

DiPaola, M. F., & Tschannen-Moran, M. (2005). Bridging or buffering? The impact of schools' adaptive strategies on student achievement. *Journal of Educational Administration, 43*(1), 60–71.

Dworkin, A. G. (1987). *Teacher burnout in the public schools: Structural causes and consequences for children.* Albany, NY: State University of New York (SUNY) Press.

Dworkin, A. G. (1997). Coping with reform: The intermix of teacher morale, teacher burnout, and teacher accountability. In B. J. Biddle, T. L. Good, & I. F. Goodson (Eds.), *International Handbook of Teachers and Teaching* (pp. 459–498). Dordrecht, The Netherlands: Kluwer.

Dworkin, A. G., Saha, L. J., & Hill, A. N. (2003). Teacher burnout and perceptions of a democratic environment. *International Educational Journal, 4*(2), 108–120.

Earl, L., Levin, B., Leithwood, K., Fullan, M., & Watson, N. (2001). *OISE/UT evaluation of the National Literacy and National Numeracy Strategies, second annual report.* Toronto, ON: Ontario Institute for Studies in Education, University of Toronto.

Esselman, M., & Moore, W. (1992, April). *In search of organizational variables which can be altered to promote an increased sense of teacher efficacy.* Paper presented at the annual meeting of the American Educational Research Association, San Francisco.

Evans, L. (1997). Understanding teacher morale and job satisfaction. *Teaching and Teacher Education, 13*(8), 831–845.

Farber, B., & Miller, J. (1981). Teacher burnout: A psycho-educational perspective. *Teachers College Record, 83*(2), 235–243.

Firestone, W., Mayrowetz, D., & Fairman, J. (1998). Performance-based assessment and instructional change: The effects of testing in Maine and Maryland. *Educational Evaluation and Policy Analysis, 20*(2), 95–113.

Ford, M. (1992). *Motivating humans: Goals, emotions, and personal agency beliefs.* Newbury Park, CA: SAGE.

Freudenberger, H. J. (1974). Staff burn-out. *Journal of Social Issues, 30*(1), 159–165.

Friedman, E. H. (1985). *Generation to generation.* New York: Guildford.

Friedman, I. A., & Farber, B. (1972). Professional self-concept as a predictor of teacher burnout. *Journal of Educational Administration, 86*(1), 28–35.

Fullan, M. (2001). *Leading in a culture of change.* San Francisco: Jossey-Bass.

Fullan, M. (2003). *The moral imperative of school leadership.* Thousand Oaks, CA: Corwin Press.

Gibson, S., & Dembo, M. H. (1984). Teacher efficacy: A construct validation. *Journal of Educational Psychology, 76*(4), 569–582.

Glickman, C. D., Gordon, S. P., & Ross-Gordon, J. M. (2001). *Supervision and instructional leadership.* Needham Heights, MA: Allyn & Bacon.

Glickman, C. D., & Tamashiro, R. T. (1982). A comparison of first-year, fifth-year, and former teachers on efficacy, ego development, and problem solving. *Psychology in Schools, 19*(4), 558–562.

Goddard, R. D. (2001). Collective efficacy: A neglected construct in the study of schools and student achievement. *Journal of Educational Psychology, 93*(3), 467–476.

Goddard, R. D., & Goddard, Y. L. (2001). A multilevel analysis of the relationship between teacher and collective efficacy in urban schools. *Teaching and Teacher Education, 17*(7), 807–818.

Goddard, R. D., Hoy, W. K., & Woolfolk Hoy, A. (2000). Collective teacher efficacy: Its meaning, measure, and impact on student achievement. *American Educational Research Journal, 37*(2), 479–507.

Goleman, D. (1994). *Emotional intelligence.* New York: Bantam.

Goleman, D. (1998). *Working with emotional intelligence.* New York: Bantam Books.

Goleman, D. (2006). *Social intelligence: The new science of human relationships.* New York: Bantam Dell.

Goodlad, J. I. (1984). *A place called school: Prospects for the future.* New York: McGraw-Hill.

Gray, J. (2000). *Causing concern but improving: A review of schools' experience* (Reference No. RR188). London: Department for Education and Skills.

Greenberg, L., & Paivio, S. (1997). *Working with emotions in psychotherapy.* London: Guilford.

Gronn, P. (1999). *The making of educational leaders.* London: Cassell.

Gurr, D., & Drysdale, L. (2007). Models of successful principal leadership: Victorian case studies. In C. Day & K. Leithwood (Eds.), *Successful principal leadership: An international perspective.* Dordrecht, The Netherlands: Springer.

Hackman, J., & Oldham, G. (1975). Development of the job satisfaction survey. *Journal of Applied Psychology, 60*(2), 159–170.

Hall, D. T., Schneider, B., & Nygren, H. T. (1970). Personal factors in organizational identification. *Administrative Science Quarterly, 15*(2), 176–189.

Hallinger, P. (2003). Leading educational change: Reflections on the practice of instructional and transformational leadership. *Cambridge Journal of Education, 33*(3), 329–351.

Hallinger, P., & Heck, R. (1998). Exploring the principal's contribution to school effectiveness: 1980–1995. *School Effectiveness and School Improvement, 9*(2), 157–191.

Hanushek, E. A., Kain, J. F., & Rivkin, S. G. (2001). *Why public schools lose teachers.* Cambridge, MA: National Bureau of Economic Research.

Hargreaves, A. (1998). The emotional practice of teaching. *Teaching and Teacher Education, 14*(8), 835–854.

Hargreaves, A. (2001). Emotional geographies of teaching. *Teachers College Record, 103*(6), 1056–1080.

Hargreaves, A., Beatty, B., James-Wilson, S., Lasky, S., & Schmidt, M. (in press). *The emotions of teaching and educational change.* San Francisco: Jossey-Bass.

Hargreaves, A., & Fink, D. (2006). *Sustainable Leadership.* San Francisco: Wiley and Sons.

Harris, A., & Chapman, C. (2002). *Effective leadership in schools facing challenging circumstances.* Nottingham, UK: National College for School Leadership (NCSL).

Hastings, R., & Bham, M. S. (2003). The relationship between student behaviour patterns and teacher burnout. *School Psychology International, 24*(1), 115–127.

Heneman, H. G. (1998). Assessment of the motivational reactions of teachers to a school-based performance award program. *Journal of Personnel Evaluation in Education, 12*(1), 43–59.

Herzberg, F., Mausner, B., & Snyderman, B. (1959). *The motivation to work.* New York: John Wiley & Sons.

Hipp, K. A. (1996, April). *Teacher efficacy: Influence of principal leadership behaviour.* Paper presented at the annual meeting of the American Educational Research Association, New York City.

Hipp, K. A., & Bredeson, P. V. (1995). Exploring connections between teacher efficacy and principals' leadership behavior. *Journal of School Leadership, 5*(2), 136–150.

Hirsch, E. (2004a). *Listening to the experts: A report on the 2004 South Carolina teacher working conditions survey.* Chapel Hill, NC: Southeast Center for Teaching Quality.

Hirsch, E. (2004b). *Teacher working conditions are student learning conditions: A report to Governor Mike Easley on the 2004 North Carolina teacher working conditions survey.* Chapel Hill, NC: Southeast Center for Teaching Quality.

Hochschild, A. R. (1983). *The managed heart: The commercialization of human feeling.* Berkeley & Los Angeles: University of California Press.

Hoy, W. K., & Ferguson, J. (1985). A theoretical framework and exploration of organizational effectiveness of schools. *Educational Administration Quarterly, 21*(2), 117–131.

Hoy, W. K., Tartar, J. C., & Witkoskie, L. (1992). Faculty trust in colleagues: Linking the principal with school effectiveness. *Journal of Research and Development in Education, 26*(1), 38–45.

Huberman, M. (1988). Teacher careers and school improvement. *Journal of Curriculum Studies, 20*(2), 119–132.

Huberman, M. (1993). *The lives of teachers* (2nd ed., J. Neufeld, Trans.). London: Redwood.

Ingersoll, R. (2001a). Teacher turnover and teacher shortages: An organizational analysis. *American Educational Research Journal, 38*(3), 499–534.

Ingersoll, R. (2001b). *Teacher turnover, teacher shortages, and the organization of schools.* Seattle, WA: University of Washington, Center for the Study of Teaching and Policy.

Jacobsson, C., Pousette, A., & Thylefors, I. (2001). Managing stress and feelings of mastery among Swedish comprehensive school teachers. *Scandinavian Journal of Educational Research, 45*(1), 37–53.

Johnson, S. M. (1998). Telling all sides of the truth. *Educational Leadership, 55*(7), 12–16.

Jones, E. E., & Davis, K. (1965). From acts to dispositions: The attribution process in person perception. In L. Berkowitz (Ed.), *Advances in experimental social psychology* (pp. 219–266). New York: Academic Press.

Jordan, J. V. (1993). *Challenges to connection. Work in progress No. 60.* Wellesley, MA: Stone Center Working Paper Series.

Judge, T. A., Bono, J. E., Ilies, R., & Gerhardt, M. W. (2002). Personality and leadership: A qualitative and quantitative review. *Journal of Applied Psychology 87*(4), 765–780.

Kelley, C., & Protsik, J. (1997). Risk and reward: Perspectives on the implementation of Kentucky's school-based performance award program. *Educational Administration Quarterly, 33*(4), 474–505.

Killinger, B. (1991). *Workaholics: The respectable addicts.* Toronto, ON: Key Porter.

Koch, J., & Steers, R. (1978). Job attachment, satisfaction, and turnover among public sector employees. *Journal of Vocational Behaviour, 12*(1), 119–128.

Kushman, J. (1992). The organizational dynamics of teacher workplace commitment: A study of urban elementary and middle schools. *Educational Administration Quarterly, 28*(1), 5–42.

Kyriacou, C. (2001). Teacher stress: Directions for future research. *Educational Review, 53*(1), 27–35.

Lee, V. E., Dedrick, R. F., & Smith, J. B. (1991). The effect of social organization of schools on teachers' efficacy and satisfaction. *Sociology of Education, 64*(3), 190–208.

Leithwood, K. (1994). Leadership for school restructuring. *Educational Administration Quarterly, 30*(4), 498–518.

Leithwood, K. (2005). *Teacher working conditions that matter.* Toronto, ON: Elementary Teachers' Federation of Ontario.

Leithwood, K., & Jantzi, D. (2005). A review of transformational school leadership research: 1996–2005. *Leadership and Policy in Schools, 4*(3), 177–199.

Leithwood, K., & Jantzi, D. (2006). Transformational school leadership for large-scale reform: Effects on students, teachers, and their classroom practices. *School Effectiveness and School Improvement, 17*(2), 201–227.

Leithwood, K., & Jantzi, D. (in press). Linking leadership to student learning: The role of collective efficacy. *Educational Administration Quarterly.*

Leithwood, K., Jantzi, D., & Steinbach, R. (1999). *Changing leadership for changing times.* Buckingham, UK: Open University Press.

Leithwood, K., Jantzi, D., & Steinbach, R. (2002). School leadership and teachers' motivation to implement accountability policies. *Educational Administration Quarterly, 38*(1), 94–119.

Leithwood, K., Louis, K. S., Anderson, S., & Wahlstrom, K. (2004). *How leadership influences student learning: A review of research for the Learning from Leadership Project.* New York: The Wallace Foundation.

Leithwood, K., McAdie, P., Bascia, N., & Rodrigue, A. (Eds.). (2004). *Teaching for deep understanding: Towards the Ontario curriculum we need.* Toronto, ON: Elementary Teachers' Federation of Ontario.

Leithwood, K., Menzies, T., & Jantzi, D. (1994). Earning teachers' commitment to curriculum reform. *Peabody Journal of Education, 69*(4), 38–61.

Leithwood, K., Menzies, T., Jantzi, D., & Leithwood, J. (1996). School restructuring, transformational leadership and the amelioration of teacher burnout. *Anxiety, Stress, and Coping: An International Journal, 9*(3), 199–215.

Leithwood, K., & Riehl, C. (2005). What we know about successful school leadership. In W. Firestone & C. Riehl (Eds.), *A new agenda: Directions for research on educational leadership* (pp. 22–47). New York: Teachers College Press.

Loader, D. (1997). *The inner principal.* London: Falmer.

Locke, E. A. (1976). The nature and causes of job satisfaction. In M. Dunnette (Ed.), *Handbook of industrial and organizational psychology* (pp. 1297–1349). Chicago: Rand-McNally.

Locke, E. A. (2002). The leaders as integrator: The case of Jack Welch at General Electric. In L. L. Neider & C. Schriesheim (Eds.), *Leadership* (pp. 1–22). Greenwich, CT: Information Age Publishing.

Locke, E. A., & Latham, G. P. (1984). *Goal setting: A motivational technique that works.* Englewood Cliffs: NJ: Prentice-Hall.

Locke, E. A., Latham, G. P., & Eraz, M. (1988). The determinants of goal commitment. *Academy of Management Review, 13*(1), 23–39.

Loeb, S. (2001). How teachers' choices affect what a dollar can buy: Wages and quality in K–12 schooling. In *The Teacher Workforce: Symposium Proceedings from the Education Finance Research Consortium.* Albany, NY.

Loeb, S., Darling-Hammond, L., & Luczak, J. (2005). How teaching conditions predict teacher turnover in California schools. *Peabody Journal of Education, 80*(3), 44–70.

Lortie, D. C. (1975). *School teacher: A sociological study.* Chicago: University of Chicago.

Lowe, K. B., Kroeck, K. G., & Sivasubramaniam, N. (1996). Effectiveness correlates of transformational and transactional leadership: A meta-analytical review of the MLQ literature. *Leadership Quarterly, 7*(3), 385–425.

Lumsden, L. (1998). *Teacher morale.* Eugene, OR: Clearinghouse on Educational Management. (ERIC Document Reproduction Service No. EDO-EA-98-4)

Lupton, D. (1998). *The emotional self.* London: Sage Publications.

Ma, X. (2003). Academic performance of Canadian immigrant children in reading, mathematics, and science. *Journal of International Migration and Integration, 4*(4), 541–576.

Macdonald, D. (1999). Teacher attrition: A review of the literature. *Teaching and Teacher Education, 15*(8), 835–848.

Margolis, D. R. (1998). *The fabric of self: A theory of ethics and emotions.* New Haven, CT: Yale University Press.

Marlowe, H. A. (1986). Social intelligence: Evidence for multidimensionality and construct independence. *Journal of Educational Psychology, 78*(1), 52–58.

Marlowe, B. A., & Page, M. L. (2005). *Creating and sustaining the constructivist classroom* (2nd ed.). Thousand Oaks, CA: Corwin Press.

Marzano, R. J., Waters, T., & McNulty, B. A. (2005). *School leadership that works: From research to results.* Alexandria, VA: Association for Supervision and Curriculum Development.

Mascall, B. (2003). *Leaders helping teachers helping students: The role of transformational leadership in building teacher efficacy to improve student achievement.* Unpublished doctoral dissertation, University of Toronto, Toronto, ON.

Maslach, C., & Jackson, S. E. (1981). The measurement of experienced burnout. *Journal of Occupational Behaviour, 2*(2), 99–113.

Mathieu, J., & Zajac, D. (1990). A review and meta-analysis of the antecedents, correlates, and consequences of organizational commitment. *Psychological Bulletin, 108*(2), 171–194.

Matsui, J., & Lang Research. (2005). *Bullying in the workplace: A survey of Ontario's elementary and secondary school teachers and education workers.* Toronto: Elementary Teachers' Federation of Ontario (ETFO), Ontario English Catholic Teachers' Association (OECTA), and the Ontario Secondary School Teachers' Federation (OSSTF).

Maurer, R. (1996). *Beyond the wall of resistance.* Austin, TX: Bard Books.

McLaughlin, M. W., & Mitra, D. (2001). Theory-based change and change-based theory: Going deeper, going broader. *Journal of Educational Change, 2*(4), 301–332.

Menzies, T. (1995). Teacher commitment in colleges of applied arts and technology: Sources, objects, practices, and influences. Unpublished doctoral dissertation, University of Toronto, Toronto, ON.

Miskel, C., & Ogawa, R. (1988). Work motivation, job satisfaction, and climate. In N. Boyan (Ed.), *Handbook on research on educational administration* (pp. 279–304). New York: Longman.

Møller, J., Eggen, A., Fuglestad, O. L., Langfeldt, G., Presthus, A., Skrøvset, S., et al. (2007). Successful leadership based on democratic values. In C. Day & K. Leithwood (Eds.), *Successful principal leadership: An international perspective.* Dordrecht, The Netherlands: Springer.

Mont, D., & Rees, D. I. (1996). The influence of classroom characteristics on high school teacher turnover. *Economic Inquiry, 34*(1), 152–167.

Moos, L., Krejsler, J., Kofod, K. K., & Jensen, B. B. (2007). Communicative strategies among successful Danish school principals. In C. Day & K. Leithwood (Eds.), *Successful principal leadership: An international perspective.* Dordrecht, The Netherlands: Springer.

Moriarty, V., Edmonds, S., Blatchford, P., & Martin, C. (2001). Teaching young children: Perceived satisfaction and stress. *Educational Research, 43*(1), 33–46.

Morris, J. A., Brotheridge, C. M., & Urbanski, J. C. (2005). Bringing humility to leadership: Antecedents and consequences of leader humility. *Human Relations, 58*(10), 1323–1350.

Mowday, R., Steers, R., & Porter, L. (1979). The measurement of organizational commitment. *Journal of Vocational Behaviour, 14*(2), 224–247.

Nguni, S., Sleegers, P., & Denessen, E. (2006). Transformational and transactional leadership effects on teachers' job satisfaction, organizational commitment, and organizational citizenship behavior in primary schools: The Tanzmanian case. *School Effectiveness and School Improvement, 17*(2), 145–177.

Nias, J. (1989). *Primary teachers talking: A study of teaching as work.* London: Routledge.

Nias, J., Southworth, G., & Yeomans, R. (1989). *Staff relationships in the primary school.* London: Cassell.

Nir, A. (2002). School health and its relation to teacher commitment. *Planning and Changing, 33*(1–2), 106–126.

Oatley, K., Keltner, D., & Jenkins, J. M. (2006). *Understanding emotions* (2nd ed.). Malden, MA: Blackwell.

O'Day, J. (1996). Incentives and student performance. In S. Fuhrman & J. O'Day (Eds.), *Rewards and reform: Creating educational incentives that work.* San Francisco: Jossey-Bass.

Organ, D. (1990). The motivational basis of organizational citizenship behavior. In B. M. Staw and L. Cummings (Eds.), *Research in Organizational Behavior, 12,* 43–72.

Ostroff, C. (1992). The relationship between satisfaction, attitudes, and performance: An organizational level analysis. *Journal of Applied Psychology, 77*(6), 963–974.

Ozcan, M. (1996, April). *Improving teacher performance: Toward a theory of teacher motivation.* Paper presented at the annual meeting of the American Educational Research Association, New York.

Pajares, F. (1996). Self-efficacy beliefs in academic settings. *Review of Educational Research, 66*(4), 543–579.

Parkay, F., Greenwood, G., Olejnik, S., & Proller, N. (1998). A study of the relationship among teacher efficiency, locus of control, and stress. *Journal of Research and Development in Education, 21*(4), 13–22.

Parker, K., Hannah, E., & Topping, K. J. (2006). Collective teacher efficacy, pupil attainment, and socio-economic status in primary school. *Improving Schools, 9*(2), 111–129.

Pintrich, P. R., & De Groot, E. V. (1990). Motivational and self-regulated learning components of classroom academic performance. *Journal of Educational Psychology, 82*(1), 33–40.

Pintrich, P. R., & Schunk, D. H. (2002). *Motivation in education: Theory, research, and applications* (2nd ed.). Upper Saddle River, NJ: Merrill Prentice Hall.

Pittman, T. S. (1998). Motivation. In D. T. Gilbert, S. Fiske, & G. Lindzey (Eds.), *The handbook of social psychology* (4th ed., Vol. 1, pp. 549–590). New York: McGraw-Hill.

Podsakoff, P., MacKenzie, S., Moorman, R., & Fetter, R. (1990). Transformational leader behaviors and their effects on followers' trust in leader satisfaction and organizational citizenship behaviors. *Leadership Quarterly, 1*(2), 107–142.

Pogodzinski, J. M. (2000). *The teacher shortage: Causes and recommendations for change.* Sacramento, CA: Center for California Studies, California State University.

Popper, M., & Mayseless, O. (2002). Internal world of transformational leaders. In B. Avolio & F. Yammarino (Eds.), *Transformational and charismatic leadership: The road ahead* (pp. 203–230). Oxford, UK: Elsevier Science Ltd.

Poppleton, P., Gershunsky, B., & Pullin, R. (1994). Changes in administrative control and teacher satisfaction in England and the USSR. *Comparative Education Review, 38*(3), 323–346.

Porter, L., Steers, R., Mowday, R., & Boulian, P. (1974). Organizational commitment, job satisfaction, and turnover among psychiatric technicians. *Journal of Applied Psychology, 59*(5), 603–609.

Pounder, D. (1999). Teacher teams: Exploring the job characteristics and work-related outcomes of work group enhancement. *Educational Administration Quarterly, 35*(3), 317–348.

Rafferty, M. (2002). The effects of teacher morale on teacher turnover rates. *Graduate Research Journal,* issue 2. Retrieved February 2007 from Sam Houston State University, Department of Educational Leadership and Counseling, *Graduate Research Journal* Web site: www.shsu.edu/~edu_elc/journal/Issue2/Rafferty.pdf

Reyes, P., & Imber, M. (1992). Teachers' perceptions of the fairness of their workload and their commitment, job satisfaction, and morale: Implications for teacher evaluation. *Journal of Personnel Evaluation in Education, 5*(3), 291–302.

Rhodes, C., Nevill, A., & Allan, J. (2004). Valuing and supporting teachers: A survey of teacher satisfaction, dissatisfaction, morale, and retention in an English local education authority. *Research in Education, 71*, 67–80.

Rosenblatt, Z. (2001). Teachers' multiple roles and skill flexibility: Effects on work attitudes. *Educational Administration Quarterly, 37*(5), 684–708.

Rosenholtz, S. J. (1989). *Teachers' workplace: The social organization of schools.* New York: Longman.

Rosenholtz, S. J., & Simpson, C. (1990). Workplace conditions and the rise and fall of teachers' commitment. *Sociology of Education, 63*(4), 241–257.

Ross, J. A. (1992). The antecedents and consequences of teacher efficacy. In J. Brophy (Ed.), *Advance in research on teaching* (Vol. 7, pp. 49–74). Greenwich, CT: JAI Press.

Ross, J. A. (1995). Strategies for enhancing teachers' beliefs in their effectiveness: Research on a school improvement hypothesis. *Teachers College Record, 97*(2), 227–251.

Ross, J. A. (1998). The antecedents and consequences of teacher efficacy. *Advances in Research in Teaching, 7,* 49–73.

Ross, J. A., & Gray, P. (2006). Transformational leadership and teacher commitment to organizational values. *School Effectiveness and School Improvement,* 17, 2, 179–200.

Ross, J. A., & Gray, P. (in press). Transformational leadership and teacher commitment to organizational values: The mediating effects of collective teacher efficacy. *School Effectiveness and School Improvement.*

Ross, J. A., Hogaboam-Gray, A., & Gray, P. (2004). Prior student achievement, collaborative school processes, and collective teacher efficacy. *Leadership and Policy in Schools, 3*(3), 163–188.

Ross, J. A., Hogaboam-Gray, A., & Hannay, L. (2001). Effects of teacher efficacy on computer skills and computer cognitions of Canadian students in grades K–3. *The Elementary School Journal, 102*(2), 141–162.

Ross, J. A., McKeiver, S., & Hogaboam-Gray, A. (1997). Fluctuations in teacher efficacy during implementation of destreaming. *Canadian Journal of Education, 22*(3), 283–296.

Rotter, J. B. (1966). Generalized expectancies for internal versus external control of reinforcement. *Psychological Monographs, 80*(1), 1–28.

Rotter, J. B. (1975). Some problems and misconceptions related to the construct of internal versus external control of reinforcement. *Journal of Consulting and Clinical Psychology, 43*(1), 56–67.

Rowan, B. (1996). Standards as incentives for instructional reform. In S. H. Fuhrman & J. J. O'Day (Eds.), *Rewards and reform: Creating educational incentives that work.* San Francisco: Jossey-Bass.

Salovey, P., & Mayer, D. (1990). Emotional intelligence. *Imagination, Cognition, and Personality, 9*(3), 185–211.

Sava, F. A. (2002). Causes and effects of teacher conflict-inducing attitudes towards pupils: A path analysis model. *Teaching and Teacher Education, 18*(7), 1007–1021.

Schlansker, B. (1987). A principal's guide to teacher stress. *Principal, 66*(5), 32–34.

Schnake, M. (1991). Organizational citizenship: A review, proposed model, and research agenda. *Human Relations, 44*(7), 735–759.

Schunk, D. H., & Pajares, F. (2004). Self-efficacy in education revisited: Empirical and applied evidence. In D. M. McInerney & S. Van Etten (Eds.), *Big theories revisited* (pp. 115–138). Greenwich, CT: Information Age.

Sergiovanni, T. (1967). Factors which affect satisfaction and dissatisfaction of teachers. *Journal of Educational Administration, 5*(1), 66–81.

Sergiovanni, T. (1992). *Moral leadership.* San Francisco: Jossey-Bass.

Seyfarth, J. T., & Bost, W. A. (1986). Teacher turnover and the quality of worklife in schools: An empirical study. *Journal of Research and Development in Education, 20*(1), 1–6.

Shen, J. (1997). Teacher retention and attrition from public schools: Evidence from SASS91. *Journal of Educational Research, 91*(2), 33–39.

Silins, H., & Mulford, W. (2002). Leadership and school results. In K. Leithwood & P. Hallinger (Eds.), *Second international handbook of educational leadership and administration* (pp. 561–612). Dordrecht, The Netherlands: Kluwer.

Smylie, M. A. (1990). Teacher efficacy at work. In P. Reyes (Ed.), *Teachers and their workplace*. Newbury Park, CA: SAGE.

Southworth, G. (1998). *Leading improving primary schools*. London: Falmer.

Starratt, R. J. (1991). Building an ethical school: A theory for practice in educational leadership. *Educational Administration Quarterly, 27*(2), 185–202.

Stein, M., & Spillane, J. (2005). What can researchers on educational leadership learn from research on teaching: Building a bridge. In W. Firestone & C. Riehl (Eds.), *A new agenda for research in educational leadership* (pp. 28–45). New York: Teachers College Press.

Stockard, J., & Lehman, M. B. (2004). Influences on the satisfaction and retention of 1st-year teachers: The importance of effective school management. *Educational Administration Quarterly, 40,* 742–771.

Tatar, M., & Horenczyk, G. (2003). Diversity-related burnout among teachers. *Teaching and Teacher Education, 19*(4), 397–408.

Theobald, N. D. (1990). An examination of the influence of personal, professional, and school district characteristics on public school teacher retention. *Economics of Education Review, 9*(3), 241–250.

Tschannen-Moran, M., & Barr, M. (2004). Fostering student achievement: The relationship between collective teacher efficacy and student achievement. *Leadership and Policy in Schools, 3*(3), 189–209.

Tschannen-Moran, M., & Hoy, W. K. (2000). A multidisciplinary analysis of the nature, meaning, and measurement of trust. *Review of Educational Research, 70*(4), 547–593.

Tschannen-Moran, M., & Hoy, A. W. (2001). Teacher efficacy: Capturing an elusive construct. *Teaching and Teacher Education, 17*(7), 783–805.

Tschannen-Moran, M., & Woolfolk Hoy, A. (2001). Teacher efficacy: Capturing an elusive construct. *Teaching and Teacher Education, 17*(7), 783–805.

Tschannen-Moran, M., Woolfolk Hoy, A., & Hoy, W. K. (1998). Teacher efficacy: Its meaning and measure. *Review of Educational Research, 68*(2), 202–248.

Tsui, K. T., & Cheng, Y. C. (2002). School organizational health and teacher commitment: A contingency study with multi-level analysis. *Educational Research and Evaluation, 5*(3), 249–268.

Tye, B. B., & O'Brien, L. (2002). Why are experienced teachers leaving the profession? *Phi Delta Kappan, 84*(1), 24–32.

Wang, M. C. (1983). Development and consequences of students' sense of personal control. In J. M. Levine & M. C. Wang (Eds.), *Teacher and student perceptions: Implications for learning.* Hillsdale, NJ: Erlbaum.

Waters, T., Marzano, R. J., & McNulty, B. (2003). *Balanced leadership: What 30 years of research tells us about the effect of leadership on pupil achievement. A working paper.* Aurora, CO: Mid-Continent Research for Education and Learning.

Weiner, B. (1990). On perceiving the other as responsible. In R. Dienstbier (Ed.), *Nebraska Symposium on Motivation* (Vol. 38, pp. 165–198). Lincoln: University of Nebraska Press.

Weiss, E. (1999). Perceived workplace conditions and first-year teachers' morale, career choice commitment, and planned retention: A secondary analysis. *Teacher and Teacher Education, 15*(8), 861–879.

West, M., Ainscow, M., & Stanford, J. (2005). Sustaining improvement in schools in challenging circumstances: A study of successful practice. *School Leadership and Management, 25*(1), 77–93.

Williams, L., & Hazer, J. (1986). Antecedents and consequences of satisfaction and commitment in turnover models: A reanalysis using latent variable structural equation methods. *Journal of Applied Psychology, 71*(2), 219–231.

Wright, M. D. (1991). Retaining teachers in technology education: Probable causes, possible solutions. *Journal of Technology Education, 3*(1), 55–61.

Wright, T., & Bonett, D. (2002). The moderating effects of employee tenure on the relation between organizational commitment and job performance: A meta-analysis. *Journal of Applied Psychology, 87*(6), 1183–1190.

Young, I. M. (1997). *Intersecting voices: Dilemmas of gender, political philosophy, and policy.* Princeton, NJ: Princeton University Press.

Yukl, G. (1989). *Leadership in organizations* (2nd ed.). Englewood Cliffs, NJ: Prentice Hall.

Yukl, G. (1994). *Leadership in organizations* (3rd ed.). Englewood Cliffs, NJ: Prentice-Hall.

Zaccaro, S. J., Kemp, C., & Bader, P. (2004). Leader traits and attributes. In J. Antonakis, A. T. Cianciolo, & R. J. Sternberg (Eds.), *The nature of leadership* (pp. 101–124). Thousand Oaks, CA: SAGE.

Zigarelli, M. (1996). An empirical test of conclusions from effective schools research. *Journal of Educational Research, 90*(2), 103–110.

Index

CORWIN PRESS

The Corwin Press logo—a raven striding across an open book—represents the union of courage and learning. Corwin Press is committed to improving education for all learners by publishing books and other professional development resources for those serving the field of PreK–12 education. By providing practical, hands-on materials, Corwin Press continues to carry out the promise of its motto: **"Helping Educators Do Their Work Better."**